Mediterranean Diet Cookbook Made Simple

Healthy, Easy, Quick Meals in 15 Minutes or Less.

Sherri Todd

Copyright @2024 by Sherri Todd

FIRST EDITION

Your Feedback is

Greatly Appreciated!

It's through your feedback, support and reviews that I'm able to create the best books possible and serve more people.

I would be extremely grateful if you could take just 60 seconds to kindly leave an honest review of the book on Amazon. Please share your feedback and thoughts for others to see.

To do so, simply find the book on Amazon's website (or wherever you purchased the book from) and locate the section to leave a review. Select a star rating and write a couple of sentences.

That's it! Thank you so much for your support.

Review this product

Share your thoughts with other customers

Write a customer review

Click with your camera above to get a free e-book: "Mediterranean Diet Program: Healthy Effective Weight Loss" or copy/type in
bit.ly/3YMcAr7

Table of Content

Introduction

Today, in the hustle and bustle of life, we often find it difficult to follow a balanced diet and a healthy lifestyle. In addition to our busy lifestyle, the widespread availability of ready-to-eat food has grown increasingly. We live fast and we like to eat fast, which often means, canned, over processed, deep-fried dishes, and fast-food meals, which are devoid of nutritional goodness. We also find it difficult to stay physically active since most of us work in offices where we sit in front of our desks for more than eight hours a day.

Our unhealthy eating habits and sedentary lifestyle have increased the risk of cancer, diabetes, cardiovascular diseases, obesity, and other diseases. As our health declines, our life expectancy has greatly decreased as well. We sacrifice both our physical and emotional wellbeing and forget to nourish our bodies and souls. Only when we are faced with our declining health or eminent mortality do we realize that we should have taken good care of our bodies.

Only when our health hits rock bottom do we realize that no matter how busy our lives become, we need to pause, slow down, relax, and enjoy. Well, it's not too late to change. In this respect, the Mediterranean diet helps you achieve healthy physical and emotional well-being. It is a delicious change that will turn your life around three hundred and sixty degrees. Also, the diet helps people achieve that desired healthy eating habits.

Healthy eating habits with an emphasize on habits is a term we all look up to — a healthy mind in a healthy body is our greatest achievement in terms of how we feel. The food we eat is just as important in this equation; you are what you eat. But the most important word here is "habits" a regular tendency or practice that is hard to give up. Bringing it all together; healthy eating habits, is the practice of eating healthy daily without feeling like it difficult. Thus, a diet is a lifestyle that we embrace and hold on to with much joy and willingness.

Furthermore, the Mediterranean diet is the only diet that manages to give you diversity and combine ingredients in a way that is both delicious and interesting. It helps keep the ingredient simple, the recipes easy-to-follow and cost fairly low.

Therefore, for beginners, or someone in need of something new; the Mediterranean Diet Cookbook Made Simple will inspire you to prepare quality dishes in less time. Due to peoples tight schedules, this book will help you discover new, delicious, and healthy recipes that can be prepared fast.

In addition to discovering new, healthy quick meals in less time, try incorporate the other aspects of the Mediterranean diet. That is, adding in more physical activity, making meals more social, and taking time to enjoy the small pleasures in life. As you'll learn, all of these things work together to promote a happier, healthier, and more fulfilling life.

The Mediterranean Diet and Lifestyle

The Mediterranean diet is the traditional dishes of nations bordering the Mediterranean Sea, such as France, Spain, Greece, and Italy. It is a balance of foods rich in antioxidants and healthy fats, and high in fiber. Also, the diet focuses on spending time with loved ones while preparing and enjoying meals, self-control, exercising, and reducing stress. That is where the lifestyle part comes in, caring for all aspects of your life as a whole.

Although the Mediterranean diet is a modern nutritional recommendation, this eating habit is as old as the civilizations that thrived on the banks of the Nile River, the Mediterranean region where the ancient yet advanced civilizations arose. Along with the progress of history, the customs, cultures, religions, languages, thinking, and lifestyle of the Mediterranean region also flourished. The diverse cultures integrated with one another and the eating habits merged.

However, the actual origins of the Mediterranean diet are lost in time. The passing of history has made various developments and changes in the eating habits of the people in the Mediterranean region. Despite this, the importance of vegetables as the major component of the Mediterranean traditional foods was retained.

The diverse historical path, the geographical traditions and connotations that characterizes the eating habits of the countries in the Mediterranean region, and the difference between the current diet and the Mediterranean diet of our ancestors, and the introduction of the new food has given us the Mediterranean diet, as we know it today.

The modern Mediterranean diet is a healthy and nutritious eating model or plan that is closely related to the original historical, territorial, environmental, cultural, and social Mediterranean lifestyle throughout history.

Presently, the Mediterranean enhances the safety and the quality of food. This eating habit offers simple cuisine, but is rich in taste and imagination, taking advantage of all the aspects ofa healthy diet. It is an eating choice that preserves the customs and the traditions of the Mediterranean region eating habits.

The Science Behind the Mediterranean Diet

We all know that "we are what we eat." The foods we eat profoundly affect our health. Good nutrition prevents metabolic diseases, such as diabetes, obesity, hypertension, etc. and maintains good health.

The Mediterranean Diet was originally recognized as a healthy eating model by Ancel Benjamin I€eys from the University of Minnesota School of Power. As early as the 1950s, he laid the foundations for what we now refer to as the Mediterranean Diet. He also hypothesized that different dietary have different effects on health.

The discovery of the health benefits of the Mediterranean diet is also attributed to him. He was the first person to point out the relationship of the Mediterranean diet and cardiovascular disease. Keys led the famous "Seven Countries Study" which documented the relationship of cardiovascular disease and lifestyle nutrition. This study proved that health benefits of the Mediterranean diet to those who adopted it. The study showed that people who followed the Mediterranean diet had very low cholesterol and therefore, has lower risks of developing coronary heart disease.

The study showed that the mentioned findings were primarily due to the use of olive oil, vegetables, herbs and spices, pasta, bread, and other plant-based foods.

From Dr. Keys' studies, numerous scientific researchers have analyzed the relationship between chronic diseases and dietary habits. These various studies fully recognize the health benefits of the Mediterranean eating habit. Many of the former and recent clinical trials and studies have shown that the Mediterranean diet:

- Reduces the risk of metabolic syndrome and cardiovascular disease
- Decreases in abdominal circumference or belly fat
- Increases the high density lipoprotein (HDL)
- Decreases triglycerides
- Lowers blood pressure,
- Decreases glucose concentration in the blood

However, we must point out that the Mediterranean diet by itself is not able to produce the above-mentioned health benefits. Lack of physical activity and the amount of calories consumed daily by a person also affects the individual's health. Therefore, it is advised that along with adopting the Mediterranean diet, one must engage in physical activities or exercise. Dr. Keys have pointed out; the Mediterranean diet is not a diet; it is a "lifestyle".

In 1993, the European Office of the World Health Organization, the Harvard School of Public Health, and Old ways introduced the classic Mediterranean diet along with its visual representation, the Mediterranean Diet Pyramid graphic, in Cambridge Massachusetts. Using the most up-to-date nutrition study to characterize a healthy, traditional Mediterranean diet, the original Mediterranean Diet pyramid was generated based on the dietary habits of southern and Italy, Crete, and Greece circa 1960, a period when adult chronic disease was the lowest and life expectancy was the highest even though the medical services at the time were limited.

From the rudimentary Mediterranean diet pyramid, the model was updated to highlight the other vital elements of the Mediterranean diet, which emphasizes the following:

- Daily exercise
- Sharing meals with family and friends
- Nurturing a deep appreciation of delicious food and enjoyment of eating healthy

On November 2008, the Mediterranean model and diet pyramid were revisited, reviewed, and was updated to include the latest research findings. A new feature of the diet pyramid includes the addition of herbs and spices of the various Mediterranean cuisines. The placement of the shellfish and fish was also changed, recognizing the benefits of consuming them at least twice per week. A consensus from Scientific Advisory Board also updated the Mediterranean model and diet pyramid to focus on more plant-based foods in healthy eating.

Principles of the Mediterranean Diet

The diet is focused on the same core food groups you already know, but more than likely they're prepared and served in a different way. How they are eaten— more slowly, mindfully, and with family and friends—is just as important as what is eaten. The diet is based around the following eight simple principles:

Focus on vegetables: In each meal, fresh, colorful, seasonal vegetables are the stars of the plate. When you eat seasonally, you always enjoy freshness and variety.

Change your thoughts around meat: The Mediterranean diet calls for small amounts of poultry and meat, focusing instead on seafood and high-fiber legumes for protein. That doesn't mean meat is off-limits, but it's eaten in moderation, usually reserved for special occasions, and is always surrounded by vegetables.

Let herbs and spices shine: Whether they're dried or fresh, all herbs and spices add flavor, color, and tremendous health benefits to your meals.

Embrace healthy fats: Mediterranean is not synonymous with low fat. Instead, it features healthy, high-quality sources of fat. Olive oil is a staple ingredient in every kitchen, along with nuts, seeds, and olives.

Enjoy quality dairy foods: Unsweetened plain or Greek yogurt and cheese are traditional in the Mediterranean diet. However, like meat, they're eaten in smaller amounts and usually alongside fruits, vegetables, and other staple foods.

Switch to ancient grains: Instead of white or refined grains, which have been stripped of their nutrients, the Mediterranean diet features whole and cracked ancient grains like farro, barley, oats, and bulgur. Bread is a staple, but it's made with whole grains and is often a fermented sourdough.

Highlight fruit as your dessert: Fruits are full of natural sugars, and when served along with some nuts, a small portion of cheese, or baked into a dessert, they add fiber and nutrients while satisfying your sweet tooth.

Make meals a celebration: Mediterranean meals aren't about gourmet dining. They're about celebrating the simplicity of food and taking time to enjoy its fresh Oavors with friends and family. Whenever possible, sit down at the table with someone you care about and take time to appreciate your meal and where it came from.

The Mediterranean Diet Food Pyramid

The Mediterranean diet food pyramid was designed by the Harvard School of Public Health, the World Health Organization, and Old Ways Preservation Trust, a food and nutrition non-profit organization. It's a visual guideline that makes the principles of the diet easy to understand and follow.

Vegetables, fruits, whole grains, olive oil, legumes, nuts, seeds, herbs, and spices make up the base or the widest part of the pyramid, because these are foods to eat at every meal.

Seafood, especially oily fish, occupies the next level and should be eaten often, or at least twice each week. Poultry, eggs, cheese, and yogurt follow, with a guideline of eating moderate portions daily to weekly.

The smallest part of the pyramid represents meat and sweets, which should be enjoyed less often and reserved for special occasions.

Water is the beverage of choice. However, if you enjoy red wine, it does have some heart health benefits when consumed in moderation—although it may not be appropriate for everyone.

Healthy benefits of Mediterranean diet

Since we have discovered the findings of Dr. Ancel Keys "Seven Countries Study" that showed people whose diet comprised mostly of vegetables, fruits, grains, beans, and fish were among the healthiest. Thus, if healthy living is your desire, it will be helpful to get a look at the big picture.

Scientists have studied the characteristics of the Mediterranean diet for more than a century now. In the following years, numerous scientific evidences support the healthfulness of the Mediterranean diet.

- **Healthy and long life**
  The Mediterranean cuisine is often referred to as the healthiest cuisine in the world and the diet doesn't stray too far away. Being based mostly on fresh

vegetables and fruits, healthy oils and whole grains, as well as lean meat and seafood, it's not hard to see why this diet is considered this healthy. Combine it with a glass of red wine and you've got yourself a fun, easy going diet.

- **Heart** Health

Scientific evidence easily connects a good heart health with certain foods, mainly vegetables, fruits, olive oil and nuts. And the Mediterranean diet has it all!

- **Weight Loss**

Although the main focus of this diet is not weight loss, it will surely help with it if that's what you're looking for. Just look at it from this point of view: fresh, clean food combined with whole grains, good fats, less sugar and plenty of liquids and exercise. You have all the ingredients for an evident weight loss.

- **Controls diabetes**

Because it focuses on fresh ingredients and it packs plenty of vitamins, antioxidants and minerals, this diet is a great way to keep your diabetes under control.

- **Retaining your mobility.**

Muscle weakness and other signs of frailty are reduced by 70% in the elderly who follow a Mediterranean diet.

- **No risks involved**

The Mediterranean diet is one of the most balanced diets, therefore there are no risks involved as long as you eat everything with moderation, do plenty of exercise and drink as much liquids as you can.

- It is affordable

The Mediterranean diet is accessible even if you're on a budget. Beans, vegetables, fruits, herbs and whole grains as well as a good quality olive oil are not as expensive as they sound, but they offer so many cooking options.

- Increasing life expectancy.

  Those who follow a Mediterranean diet have a 20% lower risk of developing heart disease or cancer and a 20% lower overall mortality rate.

- Cardiovascular disease and stroke prevention.

  Reducing the amount of refined bread, processed foods, and red meat you eat, as well as encouraging the use of red wine instead of hard liquor, are all things you can do to help prevent heart disease and stroke.

Important Rules to Follow Mediterranean Diet Guidelines

What comes to mind when you hear Mediterranean?! You'd probably say exactly what most people would: feta cheese, tomatoes, peppers, basil and olives, but a true Mediterranean diet is far more complex and versatile and offers way more options that a regular Mediterranean cuisine restaurant does.

The guidelines of the Mediterranean diet are:

- Eat vegetables as many times a day as possible, both raw and cooked, but avoid potatoes as their nutritional content is less than other veggies.
- Eat fresh fruits multiple times a day, either whole or in juices or smoothies.
- Include fresh herbs in your cooking, both for their flavor, but also for their health benefits.
- Focus on whole grains, using them in breads or buns or even in desserts.
- Olive oil is the main cooking oil – except for deep frying, although this particular way of cooking is not something found very often in the Mediterranean diet.
- Find daily snacks for your cravings, such as nuts and dried fruits.
- Fish and seafood are highly recommended a few times a week.
- Meat is allowed, but focus on lean meat and avoid salami or other deli delicacies.
- Dairy products are allowed – yogurt and buttermilk are a great addition to your diet.
- Butter is great, but less is more! – Refined sugar is allowed but in low quantities.

- A glass of red wine is more than welcomed.

I(eep in mind that these are the Mediterranean diet guidelines to achieve a successful results of the healthy life. These rules are not just a set of random things to adhere to though; they are backed up by scientific evidence and common sense. No sacrifice has to be made in order to achieve the aimed result!

Food restrictions

What to eat:

Ideally, you should eat a Mediterranean diet consisting of these healthful foods:

- **Vegetables:** Onions, cauliflower, potatoes, sweet potatoes, turnips, carrots, tomatoes, broccoli, kale, spinach, Brussels sprouts, and cucumbers.
- **Fruits:** Pears, strawberries, peaches, grapes, apples, bananas, oranges, dates, figs, melons
- **Nuts, seeds, and nut butter:** Almond butter, peanut butter, hazelnuts, cashews, almonds, walnuts, macadamia nuts, sunflower seeds, pumpkin seeds
- **Legumes:** Peanuts, chickpeas, beans, peas, lentils, pulses
- **Whole grains:** Brown rice, buckwheat, oats, rye, barley, corn, whole wheat bread, and pasta Fish and seafood: Trout, tuna, mackerel, shrimp, salmon, sardines, oysters, clams, crab, mussels
- **Poultry:** Turkey, chicken, duck, Eggs: Q_uail, chicken, and duck eggs

- **Dairy:** cheese, yogurt, milk

- **Herbs and spices:** Garlic, basil, sage, nutmeg, cinnamon, pepper, mint, rosemary

- **Healthy fats:** olives, avocados, extra virgin olive oil, and avocado oil.

Foods to limit:

When following a Mediterranean diet, it's important to avoid foods and substances that have been processed or refined:

- **Added sugar:** Many foods have added sugar, but soda, candy, ice cream, table sugar, syrup, and baked products contain the most.

- **Refined grains:** Tortillas, chips, crackers, white bread, pasta

- **Trans fats:** Fried foods, margarine, and other processed foods Refined oils: soybean oil, cottonseed oil, grapeseed oil, canola oil

- **Processed meat:** Deli meats, processed sausages, hot dogs, beef jerky

- **Highly processed foods:** Microwave popcorn, fast food, convenience meals, granola bars

Eating Out on the Mediterranean Diet

Eating out on the Mediterranean diet is very easy, and the trend toward healthier menus and vegetarian and vegan offerings makes it easier than ever before. Some of the best restaurants for the Mediterranean diet are seafood houses, farm-to-table establishments, and Italian, Spanish, Greek, and Proven3al (Southern French) restaurants. Vegetarian restaurants also offer a wide variety of delicious pasta dishes and entrées that are made healthfully and with fresh ingredients.

Here are a few guidelines to follow when dining out on the Mediterranean diet:

- Go easy on the bread basket. Although bread is welcomed on the Mediterranean diet, you don't want to add too many calories to your meal before your entrée hits the table. When you do eat bread, ask that olive oil and pepper be brought to the table instead of butter.

- Order food that is broiled, baked, sautéed (in olive oil, not butter), grilled, braised, roasted, poached, or steamed. Avoid any entrée that is breaded or deep- fried.

- Try to include a fresh salad with your meal, but skip the creamy dressings. Instead, ask for vinaigrette or olive oil and vinegar.

- If you order a meat entrée, chances are that the portion will be much larger than those favored on the Mediterranean diet. This is also usually true when having pasta. If this is the case, ask the server to either box half of it up before serving you or to bring you a carryout box along with the entrée. Then just put about half of the portion into the box before you start eating and enjoy it another day. This will stretch your dollar without stretching your waistline.

- For the most part, opt for fruit or a cheese plate for dessert. Other good choices for a sweet treat are sorbet and baked fruit dishes. By all means, have a piece of chocolate cake or a creme brûlée now and then, but make it a rare treat and share it with someone or take half of it home.

The Mediterranean diet is all about enjoying great food in pleasant surroundings and with wonderful people. This makes restaurant dining a natural part of the diet, so try not to stress too much about where and what to eat. Most restaurants have plenty of Mediterranean friendly choices.

Meal Planning

Deciding what to eat every day can be a tedious task. Life is already busy. Work, family, and social responsibilities can make life hectic. Adding what to eat to that long list of tasks can make your head explode. Most times, people end up tossing ingredients together for a quick meal or ordering takeout. However, meal planning is an easy way to solve what you should eat for dinner.

What Is Meal Planning?

In short, meal planning involves creating a weekly menu of what you will eat. In other words, meal planning takes the guessing out of cooking or deciding what's for dinner. Meal planning also has several benefits. For example, meal planning can be beneficial for persons who want to drop a few pounds or lower their cholesterol. Meal planning can also help people stick to a food budget or plan meals for their whole family. Meal planning can also help athletes monitor the nutrients they consume. This way, they can increase or decrease their intake of certain foods.

Tips to Help Plan your Meal

Meal planning sounds extremely simple. However, it can quickly become complicated, especially if you are a newbie. Use these tips to help your meal plan like an expert.

Ask Your Loved Ones: Although it sounds obvious, asking what your family wants to eat can be extremely helpful. You can easily get caught up in what you want to eat instead of what everybody else in your house wants. This way, people are more likely to eat what you prepare since the meal plan contains a dish for everyone.

Use A **Calendar:** Once you've got everyone's opinions on what they want to eat, put the information on a calendar. The calendar can contain meals for the week, a few weeks, or even a month. You can use a digital calendar or purchase a physical calendar, fill in the spots, and hang it in your kitchen.

Plan Theme Nights: Planning theme nights can make meals interesting. While it maybe annoying to some people, if you've got kids, it can be the perfect way to get them interested in nutrient-dense foods. For example, meatless Mondays, fish Tuesdays, bulgar Wednesdays, brown rice Thursdays, and pizza Fridays are excellent themes for the week.

Use Shopping Lists: Shopping lists help you stay on task and minimize the chances of purchasing foods you do not eat. Look at the recipes you intend to cook and write down the ingredients. You can use a blank index card or shopping list template or type your shopping lists on your phone or laptop. Once you've got your shopping lists, you can choose a shopping day.

Leftovers: It's important to incorporate leftovers when meal planning. Some people like to cook larger portions to eat them all week long, while others only eat leftovers the day after. Furthermore, some people do not consume leftovers. This information will prevent you from cooking too much or too little food.

Prep Immediately: Away Once you have purchased your ingredients, start prepping them as soon as you get home. Chop the onions, celery, and garlic. Wash your fruits and vegetables. Roast your eggplants in the oven, and make your granola bars. Prepping the foods right away will minimize the work you have to do over the period of the week.

Cook Parts of Your Meal: Take it a step further and start cooking your meal. For example, roast the veggies if you are making a bowl that calls for roasted vegetables. If you are making quinoa fruit salad, cook the quinoa and store it in the fridge overnight. When you are ready to assemble the quinoa salad, you won't have to wait for the quinoa to cool down. You can just toss the fruit salad ingredients together.

Freezing Meals: The freezer plays a critical role in meal planning. You can make double batches of pecan cherry zucchini bread or cashew butter buckeye balls and freeze them. Most foods like soups can be frozen for up to a month, so you won't have to reheat foods. You can simply defrost the frozen food, reheat it, and it will be just like new!

Breakfast

Pumpkin Pie Parfait

Ingredients (*Cook time: 0 minutes*)

- 1 (15-ounce/ 425-g) can pure pumpkin purée
- 4 teaspoons honey
- 1 teaspoon pumpkin pie spice
- ¼ teaspoon ground cinnamon
- 2 cups plain Greek yogurt
- 1 cup honey granola

Methods (*Servings 4*)

1. Combine the pumpkin purée, honey, pumpkin pie spice, and cinnamon in a large bowl and stir to mix well.
2. Cover the bowl with plastic wrap and chill in the refrigerator for at least 2 hours.
3. Make the parfaits: Layer each parfait glass with ¼ cup pumpkin mixture in the bottom.
4. Top with ¼ cup of yogurt and scatter each top with ¼ cup of honey granola. Repeat the layers until the glasses are full. Serve immediately.

Per Serving

calories: 263 fats: 8.9g protein: 15.3g carbs: 34.6g fiber: 6.0g

Quinoa Breakfast

Ingredients (*Cook time: 15 minutes*)

- 5 dried apricots, finely chopped
- 2 tablespoons honey

- 2 dried dates, pitted, finely chopped
- 2 cups milk, low-fat
- 1/4 cup raw almonds, chopped
- 1 teaspoon sea salt
- 1 teaspoon ground cinnamon
- 1 cup quinoa 1 teaspoon vanilla extract

Methods *(Servings 4)*

1. In a skillet, toast the almonds over medium heat for about 3-5 minutes or until just golden; set aside.
2. In a saucepan, heat the quinoa and the cinnamon over medium heat until warmed through.
3. Add the milk and sat, stir, bring to boil, reduce the heat to low, and cover; simmer for 15 minutes.
4. Stir in the apricots, dates, honey, and vanilla and half of the almonds. Transfer into a bowl and top with the remaining almonds; serve.

Per Serving

calories: 321 fats: 2 g protein: 12 g carbs: 51.7 g fiber: 5.2 g

Ricotta Toast with Strawberries

Ingredients *(Cook time: 0 minutes)*

- ½ cup crumbled ricotta cheese
- 1 tablespoon honey, plus additional as needed
- Pinch of sea salt, plus additional as needed
- 4 slices of whole-grain bread, toasted
- 1 cup sliced fresh strawberries
- 4 large fresh basil leaves, sliced into thin shreds

Methods (Servings 2)

1. Mix together the cheese, honey, and salt in a small bowl until well incorporated.
2. Taste and add additional salt and honey as needed. Spoon 2 tablespoons of the cheese mixture onto each slice of bread and spread it all over.
3. Sprinkle the sliced strawberry and basil leaves on top before serving.

Per Serving

calories: 274 fats: 7.9g protein: 13.1g carbs: 39.8g[ther: $.0g

Pesto Portobello Omelet

Ingredients (Cook time: 1$ minutes)

- 4 egg whites (or 3 eggs)
- 1 Portobello mushroom cap, sliced
- 1/4 cup mozzarella cheese, low-fat, shredded
- 1/4 cup red onion, chopped
- 1 teaspoon prepared pesto
- 1 teaspoon olive oil
- 1 teaspoon water
- Salt and ground black pepper, to taste

Methods (Servings 1)

1. In a skillet, heat the olive oil over medium heat. Add the mushrooms and the onion; cook for about 3-5 minutes until the mushrooms are soft.
2. In a small bowl, whisk the water and the egg whites together and pour over the mushrooms and onions in the skillet.
3. Season with salt and pepper; cook for about 5 minutes, occasionally stirring, until the egg whites are no longer runny.

4. Sprinkle mozzarella over and top with pesto. Fold the omelet in half; continue cooking for about 2-3 minutes or until the cheese melts.

Per serving:

calories 241, fat 12.3 g, protein 25.9 g, carb. 7.9 g, fiber 1.6 g.

Morning Overnight Oats with Raspberries

Ingredients (*Cook time: 0 minutes*)

- ⅔ cup unsweetened almond milk
- ¼ cup raspberries
- ⅓ cup rolled oats
- 1 teaspoon honey
- ¼ teaspoon turmeric
- ⅛ teaspoon ground cinnamon
- Pinch ground cloves

Methods (*Servings 2*)

1. Place the almond milk, raspberries, rolled oats, honey, turmeric, cinnamon, and cloves in a mason jar.
2. Cover and shake to combine.
3. Transfer to the refrigerator for at least 8 hours, preferably 24 hours. Serve chilled.

Per Serving

calories: 81 fats: 1.9g protein: 2.1g carbs: 13.8g fiber: 3.0g

- 1 cup almond milk
- 1 cup water
- Pinch sea salt
- 1 cup old-fashioned oats
- ½ cup dried cranberries
- 1 teaspoon ground cinnamon

Methods *(Servings 2)*

1. In a medium saucepan over high heat, bring the almond milk, water, and salt to a boil.
2. Stir in the oats, cranberries, and cinnamon. Reduce the heat to medium and cook for 5 minutes, stirring occasionally.
3. Remove the oatmeal from the heat. Cover and let it stand for 3 minutes.
4. Stir before serving

Per Serving

calories: 107 fats: 2.1g protein: 3.2g carbs: 18.2g fiber: 4.1g

Creamy Breakfast Bulgur with Berries

Ingredients *(Cook time: 10 minutes)*

- ½ cup medium-grain bulgur wheat
- 1 cup water
- Pinch sea salt
- ¼ cup unsweetened almond milk
- 1 teaspoon pure vanilla extract
- ¼ teaspoon ground cinnamon
- 1 cup fresh berries of your choice

Methods *(Servings 2)*

Fennel Bruschetta

Ingredients *(Cook time: 10 minutes)*

- 6 large-sized tomatoes, diced
- 2 garlic cloves, minced
- 1/4 cup olive oil, extra-virgin, for brushing
- 1/3 cup fresh basil, minced
- 1/2 large Bermuda onion, diced
- 1 loaf (20 ounces) French bread, sliced into ½ -inch thick pieces
- 1½ tablespoons fennel seed
- 1/3 cup olive oil, extra-virgin
- Salt and black pepper, to taste

Methods *(Servings 20)*

1. In a mixing bowl, combine the tomatoes, fennel seeds, garlic, onion, basil, the 1/3 cup of olive oil, and season of salt and then pepper. Refrigerate for a minimum of 1 hour to allow the flavors to blend.
2. Preheat the oven to 350F.
3. Brush the sides of the slices of bread with a little of the1/4 cup olive oil. Place them into baking sheet, and toast for 3 minutes each side until golden brown.
4. To serve, scoop the chilled tomato toppings into each toasted bread slice, arrange them on a serving plate.

Per serving:

calories 146, fat 6.6 g, 0 mg, protein 4 g, carb. 18.8 g, fiber1.6 g.

Cinnamon Oatmeal with Dried Cranberries

Ingredients *(Cook time: 8 minutes)*

1. Put the bulgur in a medium saucepan with the water and sea salt, and bring to a boil.
2. Cover, remove from heat, and let stand for 10 minutes until water is absorbed.
3. Stir in the milk, vanilla, and cinnamon until fully incorpo-rated.
4. Divide between 2 bowls and top with the fresh berries to serve.

Per Serving

calories: 173 fats: 1.6g protein: 3.kg carbs: 34.0gJiber: 6.0g

Greek Omelet

Ingredients (Cook time: 10 minutes)

- 4 large eggs
- 1/4 cup spinach, cooked
- 2 teaspoons extra-virgin olive oil
- 2 tablespoons fresh dill, chopped
- 2 scallions, thinly sliced
- 1/2 cup (2 ounces) feta cheese, crumbled
- Freshly ground pepper, to taste

Methods (Servings 2)

1. Remove any excess water from the cooked spinach by squeezing.
2. In a medium mixing bowl, beat the eggs. Add the feta, spinach, scallions, pepper, and dill; with a rubber spatula, mix gently to combine.
3. Place the rack 4 inches from the source of heat and preheat broiler.
4. In a 10-inch non-stick skillet, heat the oil over medium heat. Pour the egg mixture, tilting the skillet to distribute evenly. Reduce the heat to medium-low; cook for about 3-4 minutes, lifting the edges and allow the uncooked egg to Oow underneath, until the bottom of the mixture is light golden.

5. Transfer the skillet to the preheated broiler; broil for about 1 1/2-2 1/2 minutes, or until the top is set.
6. Slide the omelet onto a platter, cut into wedges, and serve.

Per serving:

calories 267, fat 19 g, protein 19 g, carb 4 g., fiber 2 g.

Banana Corn Fritters

Ingredients *(Cook time: 10 minutes)*

- ½ cup yellow cornmeal
- ¼ cup flour
- 2 small ripe bananas, peeled and mashed
- 2 tablespoons unsweetened almond milk
- 1 large egg, beaten
- ½ teaspoon baking powder
- ¼ to ½ teaspoon ground chipotle chili
- ¼ teaspoon ground cinnamon
- ¼ teaspoon sea salt
- 1 tablespoon olive oil

Methods *(Servings 2)*

1. Stir together all ingredients except for the olive oil in a large bowl until smooth.
2. Heat a non-stick skillet over medium-high h eat. Add the olive oil and drop about 2 tablespoons of batter for each fritter.
3. Cook for 2 to 3 minutes until the bottoms are golden brown, then flip.
4. Continue cooking for 1 to 2 minutes more, until cooked through.
5. Repeat with the remaining batter. Serve warm.

Per Serving

calories: 396 fats: 10.6g protein: 7.3g carbs: 68.0g fiber: 4.8g

Egg-Feta Scramble

Ingredients (Cook time: 1$ minutes)

- 6 eggs 3/4 cup crumbled feta cheese
- 2 tablespoons green onions, minced
- 2 tablespoons red peppers, roasted, diced
- 1/4 teaspoon kosher salt
- 1/4 teaspoon garlic powder
- 1/4 cup Greek yogurt
- 1/2 teaspoon dry oregano
- 1/2 teaspoon dry basil
- 1 teaspoon olive oil
- A few cracks freshly ground black pepper
- Warm whole-wheat tortillas, optional

Methods (Servings 4)

1. Preheat a skillet over medium heat. In a bowl, whisk the eggs, the sour cream, basil, oregano, garlic powder, salt, and pepper. Gently add the feta.
2. When the skillet is hot, add the olive oil and then the egg mixture; allow the egg mix to set then scrape the bottom of the pan to let the uncooked egg to cook. Stir in the red peppers and the green onions.
3. Continue cooking until the eggs mixture is cooked to your preferred doneness. Serve immediately.
4. If desired, sprinkle with extra feta and then wrap the scrambled eggs in tortillas.

Per serving:

calories 260, fat 16 g protein 16 g carb 12 g Jibcr> *1 g.*

Ricotta Tartine and Honey-Roasted Cherry

Ingredients (*Cook time: 15 minutes*)

- 4 slices (1/2-inch-thick) artisan bread, whole-grain
- 2 cups fresh cherries, pitted
- 2 teaspoons extra-virgin olive oil
- 1/4 cup slivered almonds, toasted
- 1 teaspoon lemon zest
- 1 teaspoon fresh thyme
- 1 tablespoon lemon juice
- 1 tablespoon honey, plus more for serving
- 1 cup ricotta cheese, part-skim
- Pinch of flaky sea salt, such as Maldon
- Pinch of salt

Methods (*Servings 4*)

1. Preheat oven to 400F. Line a rimmed baking sheet with parchment paper; set aside.
2. In a mixing bowl, toss the cherries with the honey, oil, lemon juice, and salt. Transfer into pan. Roast for about 15 minutes, shaking the pan once or twice during roasting, until the cherries are very soft and warm.
3. Toast the bread. Top with the cheese, the cherries, thyme, lemon zest, almonds, and season with sea salt. If desired, drizzle more honey.
4. *Notes:* Toast the cherries and refrigerate for up to 3 days. When ready to serve, just reheating.

Per serving:

calories 320, fat 13 g, protein 15 g, carb 39 g., fiber 6 g.

Orange Cardamom Buckwheat Pancakes

Ingredients *(Cook time: 10 minutes)*

- ½ cup buckwheat flour
- ½ teaspoon cardamom
- ½ teaspoon baking powder
- ¼ teaspoon baking soda
- ½ cup milk
- ¼ cup plain Greek yogurt
- 1 egg
- ½ teaspoon orange extract
- 1 tablespoon maple syrup (optional)

Methods *(Servings 2)*

1. In a medium bowl, combine the buckwheat flour, cardamom, baking powder, and baking soda.
2. In another bowl, combine the milk, yogurt, egg, orange extract, and maple syrup (if using) and whisk well to combine.
3. Add the wet ingredients to the dry ingredients and stir until the batter is smooth.
4. Heat a non-stick skillet or a griddle over high heat. When the pan is hot, reduce the heat to medium.
5. Pour the batter into the pan to make four 6-inch pancakes. Depending on the size of your pan, you may need to do this in four batches.

Per Serving:

calories: 196; fat: 6g; protein: 10g; carbs: 27g; fiber: 3g.

Mediterranean Breakfast Pizza

Ingredients *(Cook time: 15 minutes)*

- 2 (6- to 8-inch-long) pieces of whole-wheat naan bread
- 2 tablespoons prepared pesto
- 1 medium tomato, sliced
- 2 large eggs

Methods (Servings 2

1. Heat a large non-stick skillet over medium-high heat. Place the naan bread in the skillet and let it warm for about 2 minutes on each side. The bread should be softened and just starting to turn golden.
2. Spread 1 tablespoon of the pesto on one side of each slice. Top the pesto with tomato slices to cover. Remove the pizzas from the pan and place each one on its own plate.
3. Crack the eggs into the pan, keeping them separated, and cook until the whites are no longer translucent and the yolk is cooked to desired doneness.
4. With a spatula, spoon one egg onto each pizza.

Per Serving:

calories: 427; fat: 17g; protein: 17g; carbs: 10g; fiber: $g.

Power Peach Smoothie Bowl

Ingredients (Cook time: 1$ minutes)

- 2 cups packed partially thawed frozen peaches
- '/2 cup plain or vanilla Greek yogurt
- '/2 ripe avoCado
- 2 tablespoons flax meal
- 1 teaspoon vanilla extract
- 1 teaspoon orange extract
- 1 tablespoon honey (optional)

Methods *(Servings 2)*

1. Combine all of the ingredients in a blender and blend until smooth.
2. Pour the mixture into two bowls, and, if desired, sprinkle with additional toppings.

Per Serving:

Calories: 213; fat: 13g; Protein: 6g; carbs: 23g; Fiber: 7g.

Spinach, Sun-Dried Tomato, And Feta Egg Wraps

Ingredients *(Cook time: 7 minutes)*

- 1 tablespoon olive oil
- ¼ cup minced onion
- 3 to 4 tablespoons minced sun-dried tomatoes in olive oil and herbs
- 3 large eggs, beaten
- 1½ cups packed baby spinach
- 1 ounce crumbled feta cheese
- Salt
- 2 (8-inch) whole-wheat tortillas

Methods *(Servings 2)*

1. In a large skillet, heat the olive oil over medium-high heat. Add the onion and tomatoes and sauté for about 3 minutes.
2. Turn the heat down to medium. Add the beaten eggs and stir to scramble them.
3. Add the spinach and stir to combine. Sprinkle the feta cheese over the eggs. Add salt to taste.
4. Warm the tortillas in the microwave for about 20 seconds each.
5. Fill each tortilla with half of the egg mixture. Fold in half or roll them up and serve.

calories: 435; fat: 28g; protein: 17g; carbs: 31g; fiber: 6g.

Fruity Breakfast Couscous

Ingredients (*Cook time: 15 minutes*)

- 1 cinnamon stick
- 3 cups milk
- 1/4 tsp. Himalayan salt
- 2 tbsp. raw honey (extra for serving)
- 1/4 cup dried raisins
- 1/2 cup dried apricots, chopped
- 1 cup raw whole-wheat couscous
- 4 tsp. melted butter

Methods (*Servings 4*)

1. In a pot, add the milk and cinnamon. Simmer, but do not boil.
2. Remove it from the heat. Whisk in the couscous, apricots, raisins, honey, and salt.
3. Cover the pot. Set aside for 15 minutes.
4. Drizzle with butter and serve.

Per Serving:

calories: 333 fats: 8g protein: 12g carbs: 54g

Spanish-Style Toasted Tomato Baguettes

Ingredients (*Cook time: 8 minutes*)

- 2 baguettes, halved lengthwise
- 4 tsp. crushed garlic
- 2 ripe heirloom tomatoes, grated
- 2 tbsp. extra-virgin olive oil
- 4 thin slices of smoked ham
- Freshly ground black pepper
- 1 tsp. flaky sea salt

Methods (*Servings 4*)

1. Place a wire rack in the center of the oven and preheat to 500F.
2. Toast the baguette halves for 6 to 8 minutes, or until crispy.
3. Then spread 1 tsp. of crushed garlic over the face of each baguette.
4. Top the garlic with a tomato.
5. Sprinkle each baguette with oil and top each with a slice of ham. Season with salt and pepper to taste.

Per Serving:

Calories: 267 Fat: 15g Protein: 18g Carbs: 15g

Salmon & Swiss Chard Crepes

Ingredients (*Cook time: 15 minutes*)

- 1 cup fresh Swiss chard, chopped
- 1 tbsp. flax meal
- 1 tbsp. nutritional yeast
- 1/4 tsp. crushed dried thyme
- 1 small bunch of fresh parsley, chopped
- Himalayan salt
- Freshly ground black pepper
- 2 large free-range eggs

- 2 tsp. extra-virgin olive oil
- 3oz. wild smoked salmon
- '/2 large Hass avocado, sliced
- 2 tbsp. feta, crumbled
- 1 tsp. fresh lemon juice

Methods (Servings 2

1. In a blender, add parsley, thyme, yeast, flax meal, and Swiss chard.
2. Season with salt and pepper and blend until the chard is fine.
3. Add the eggs and mix again. Heat oil in a pan. Spread half of the chard mixture evenly. Cook for 3 minutes.
4. Top the crepe with half of the feta, avocado, and salmon.
5. Drizzle with lemon juice and repeat with the remaining ingredients. Serve.

Per Serving:

Calories: 679 fat: 49.2g Protein: 44.4g Carbs: 6.6g

Pasta and Grains

Pasta with Cashew Sauce

Ingredients *(Cook time: 15 minutes)*

- 2 oz. fresh arugula
- ½ cup peas
- 1½ cups broccoli florets
- 1 small white onion, diced
- 1 Tbsp. extra-virgin olive oil
- Salt and black pepper, to taste
- 4 cherry tomatoes/sun-dried tomatoes, halved
- 4 oz. whole wheat cannelloni pasta

Sauce:

- ½ cup fresh basil
- ½ cup roasted cashews
- 2 garlic cloves
- 2 Tbsp. lemon juice
- ¼ tsp. sea salt
- ½ cup water

Methods *(Servings 2)*

1. Cook pasta following the package directions. Just before the pasta is done, add in the broccoli florets as it finishes cooking. Take out 1 cup of pasta water, drain, and set aside.
2. Meanwhile, prepare your sauce. Combine all the ingredients in the blender until smooth.

3. Heat the oil in a frying pan on medium heat. Add bell peppers, onion, and seasonings and sauté until tender. Stir in sun-dried tomatoes and arugula and cook for 3 minutes.
4. Toss in the pasta with broccoli. Pour the sauce and add some pasta water for desired consistency. Cook for 4 minutes, stirring occasionally.
5. Garnish with grated hard cheese, if desired.

Per serving:

calories: $63, fat: 23 g protein: 19 g carbs: 73 g fiber: 10 g

Tomato Linguine

Ingredients (Cook time: 10 minutes)

- 8 ounces whole-grain linguine
- 1 tablespoon olive oil
- '/4 cup yellow onion, chopped
- 1 teaspoon fresh oregano, chopped
- 2 garlic cloves, minced
- 1 teaspoon tomato paste
- '/2 teaspoon salt
- '/4 teaspoon freshly ground black pepper
- 8 ounces' cherry tomatoes, halved
- '/2 cup Parmesan cheese, grated
- 1 tablespoon fresh parsley, chopped

Methods (Servings 4)

1. Bring a pot of water to a boil over high heat. Add the linguine to the pot and cook 9 minutes or until al dente. Transfer the linguine to a plate, and reserve '/2 cup of the linguine water.

2. Heat the olive oil in a non-stick skillet over medium-high heat. Add the onion, oregano, and garlic to the skillet and sauté for 5 minutes until the onion is translucent.
3. Add the tomato paste, linguine water to the skillet, and sprinkle with salt and pepper. Stir to combine well and cook for 1 more minute.
4. Add the cooked linguine and cherry tomatoes, then sauté to coat well.
5. Slide the linguine in a large plate, and pour the sauce remains in the skillet over, then spread the cheese and parsley on top before serving.

Per serving:

calories: 162 fats: 9.1g protein: 6.2g carbs: 18.1g fiber: 2.8g

Broccoli and Carrot Pasta Salad

Ingredients *(Cook time: 10 minutes)*

- 8 ounces' whole-wheat pasta
- 2 cups broccoli Oorets
- 1 cup peeled and shredded carrots
- '/4 cup plain Greek yogurt
- Juice of 1 lemon
- 1 teaspoon red pepper flakes
- Sea salt and freshly ground pepper, to taste

Methods *(Servings 2*

1. Bring a large pot of lightly salted water to a boil. Add the pasta to the boiling water and cook until al dente, about 8 to 10 minutes.
2. Drain the pasta and let rest for a few minutes.
3. When cooled, combine the pasta with the veggies, yogurt, lemon juice, and red pepper flakes in a large bowl, and stir thoroughly to combine.
4. Taste and season to taste with salt and pepper. Serve immediately.

Triple-Green Pasta

Ingredients (Cook time: 1$ minutes)

- 8 ounces uncooked penne
- 1 tablespoon extra-virgin olive oil
- 2 garlic cloves, minced
- $1/4$ teaspoon crushed red pepper
- 2 cups chopped fresh 0at-leaf(Italian) parsley, including stems
- 5 cups loosely packed baby spinach
- $1/4$ teaspoon ground nutmeg
- $1/4$ teaspoon freshly ground black pepper
- $1/4$ teaspoon kosher or sea salt
- $1/s$ cup Castelvetrano olives (or other green olives), pitted and sliced
- $1/s$ cup grated Pecorino Romano or Parmesan cheese

Methods (Servings 4)

1. In a large stockpot, cook the pasta according to the package directions, but boil 1 minute less than instructed. Drain the pasta, and save $1/4$ cup of the cooking water.
2. While the pasta is cooking, in a large skillet over medium heat, heat the oil. Add the garlic and crushed red pepper, and cook for 30 seconds, stirring constantly.
3. Add the parsley and cook for 1 minute, stirring constantly. Add the spinach, nutmeg, pepper, and salt, and cook for 3 minutes, stirring occasionally, until the spinach is wilted.
4. Add the pasta and the reserved $1/4$ cup pasta water to the skillet. Stir in the olives, and cook for about 2 minutes, until most of the pasta water has been absorbed.

5. Remove from the heat, stir in the cheese, and serve.

Per serving:

calories: 2 II; fat: 8g; protein: log; carbs: 43g; fiber: 10g

Roasted Asparagus Caprese Pasta

Ingredients (Cook time: 1$ minutes)

- 8 ounces uncooked small pasta, like orecchiette
- 1'/2 pounds fresh asparagus, ends trimmed and stalks chopped into 1-inch pieces
- 1 pint grape tomatoes, halved (about 1^1/2cups)
- 2 tablespoons extra-virgin olive oil
- '/4 teaspoon freshly ground black pepper
- '/4 teaspoon kosher or sea salt
- 2 cups fresh mozzarella, drained and cut into bite-size pieces (about 8 ounces)
- ^{1}/3 cup torn fresh basil leaves
- 2 tablespoons balsamic vinegar

Methods (Servings 6)

1. Preheat the oven to 400°F. In a large stockpot, cook the pasta according to the package directions. Drain, reserving about '/4 cup of the pasta water.
2. While the pasta is cooking, in a large bowl, toss the asparagus, tomatoes, oil, pepper, and salt together. Spread the mixture onto a large, rimmed baking sheet and bake for 15 minutes, stirring twice as it cooks.
3. Remove the vegetables from the oven, and add the cooked pasta to the baking sheet. Mix with a few tablespoons of pasta water to help the sauce become smoother and the saucy vegetables stick to the pasta.
4. Gently mix in the mozzarella and basil. Drizzle with the balsamic vinegar. Serve from the baking sheet or pour the pasta into a large bowl.

5. If you want to make this dish ahead of time or to serve it cold, follow the recipe up to step 4, then refrigerate the pasta and vegetables.
6. When you are ready to serve, follow step 5 either with the cold pasta or with warm pasta that's been gently reheated in a pot on the stove.

Per Serving:

Calories: 307; fat: 14g; Protein: 18g; Carbs: 33g; Fiber: 9g

Spaghetti with Pine Nuts and Cheese

Ingredients (Cook time: 11 minutes)

- 8 ounces' spaghetti
- 4 tablespoons almond butter
- 1 teaspoon freshly ground black pepper
- '/2 cup pine nuts
- 1 cup fresh grated Parmesan cheese, divided

Methods (Servings 4-6)

1. Bring a large pot of salted water to a boil. Add the pasta and cook for 8 minutes.
2. In a large saucepan over medium heat, combine the butter, black pepper, and pine nuts. Cook for 2 to 3 minutes, or until the pine nuts are lightly toasted. Reserve '/2cup of the pasta water.
3. Drain the pasta and place it into the pan with the pine nuts. Add ³/4cup of the Parmesan cheese and the reserved pasta water to the pasta and toss everything together to evenly coat the pasta.
4. Transfer the pasta to a serving dish and top with the remaining '/4 cup of the Parmesan cheese. Serve immediately.

Per Serving

calories: 542Jats: 32.0g protein: 20.0g carbs: 46.0g[ther: 2.0g

Pasta Puttanesca

Ingredients (Cook time: 10 minutes)

- 2 tablespoons extra-virgin olive oil
- 6 garlic cloves, finely minced (or put through a garlic press)
- 2 teaspoons anchovy paste
- '/4 teaspoon red pepper flakes, plus more as needed
- 20 black olives, pitted and chopped
- 3 tablespoons capers, drained and rinsed
- '/4 teaspoon sea salt
- '/4 teaspoon freshly ground black pepper
- 2 (14-ounce) cans crushed tomatoes, undrained
- 1 (14-ounce) can chopped tomatoes, drained
- '/4 cup chopped fresh basil leaves
- 8 ounces' whole-wheat spaghetti, cooked according to package instructions and drained

Methods (Servings 4)

1. In a sauté pan or skillet over medium heat, stir together the olive oil, garlic, anchovy paste, and red pepper flakes. Cook for about 2 minutes, stirring, until the mixture is very fragrant.
2. Add the olives, capers, sea salt, and pepper.
3. In a blender, purée the crushed and chopped tomatoes and add to the pan. Cook for about 5 minutes, stirring occasionally, until the mixture simmers.
4. Stir in the basil and cooked pasta. Toss to coat the pasta with the sauce and serve.

Per Servings

calories: 278; fat: 13g; protein: 10g; carbs: 40g; fiber: 12g

Pasta with Pesto

Ingredients *(Cook time: 0 minutes)*

- 3 tablespoons extra-virgin olive oil
- 3 garlic cloves, finely minced
- ½ cup fresh basil leaves
- ¼ cup (about 2 ounces) grated Parmesan cheese
- ¼ cup pine nuts
- 8 ounces' cooked whole-wheat pasta, drained

Methods *(Servings 4)*

1. In a blender or food processor, combine the olive oil, garlic, basil, cheese, and pine nuts. Pulse for 10 to 20 (1-second) pulses until everything is chopped and blended.
2. Toss with the hot pasta and serve.

Per Serving:

calories: 405; fat: 21g; protein: 13g; carbs: 44g; fiber: 5g

Walnut and Ricotta Spaghetti

Ingredients *(Cook time: 10 minutes)*

- 1 pound cooked whole-wheat spaghetti
- 2 tablespoons extra-virgin olive oil
- 4 cloves garlic, minced
- ¾ cup walnuts, toasted and finely chopped
- 2 tablespoons ricotta cheese

- ¼ cup flat-leaf parsley, chopped
- ½ cup grated Parmesan cheese
- Sea salt and freshly ground pepper, to taste

Methods (*Servings 6*)

1. Reserve a cup of spaghetti water while cooking the spaghetti.
2. Heat the olive oil in a non-stick skillet over medium-low heat or until shimmering. Add the garlic and sauté for a minute or until fragrant.
3. Pour the spaghetti water into the skillet and cook for 8 more minutes. Turn off the heat and mix in the walnuts and ricotta cheese.
4. Put the cooked spaghetti on a large serving plate, then pour the walnut sauce over.
5. Spread with parsley and Parmesan, then sprinkle with salt and ground pepper. Toss to serve.

Per Serving:

calories: 264 fats: 16.8g protein: 8.6g carbs: 22.8g fiber: 4.0g

Brown Rice Pilaf with Pistachios and Raisins

Ingredients (*Cook time: 15 minutes*)

- 1 tablespoon extra-virgin olive oil
- 1 cup chopped onion
- ½ cup shredded carrot
- ½ teaspoon ground cinnamon
- 1 teaspoon ground cumin
- 2 cups brown rice
- 1¾ cups pure orange juice
- ¼ cup water
- ½ cup shelled pistachios

- 1 cup golden raisins
- '/2 cup chopped fresh chives

Methods *(Servings 6)*

1. Heat the olive oil in a saucepan over medium-high heat until shimmering.
2. Add the onion and sauté for 5 minutes or until translucent. Add the carrots, cinnamon, and cumin, then sauté for 1 minutes or until aromatic.
3. Pour in the brown rice, orange juice, and water. Bring to a boil. Reduce the heat to medium-low and simmer for 7 minutes or until the liquid is almost absorbed.
4. Transfer the rice mixture in a large serving bowl, then spread with pistachios, raisins, and chives. Serve immediately

Per Serving

calories: 264 fats: 7.1g protein: 3.2g carbs: 48.9gJiber: *4.0g*

Quinoa and Chickpea Vegetable Bowls

Ingredients *(Cook time: 1$ minutes)*

- 1 cup red dry quinoa, rinsed and drained
- 2 cups low-sodium vegetable soup
- 2 cups fresh spinach
- 2 cups finely shredded red cabbage
- 1 (15-ounce/ 425-g) can chickpeas, drained and rinsed
- 1 ripe avocado, thinly sliced
- 1 cup shredded carrots
- 1 red bell pepper, thinly sliced
- 4 tablespoons Mango Sauce
- '/2 cup fresh cilantro, chopped

Mango Sauce:

- 1 mango, diced
- ¼ cup fresh lime juice
- ½ teaspoon ground turmeric
- 1 teaspoon finely minced fresh ginger
- ¼ teaspoon sea salt
- Pinch of ground red pepper
- 1 teaspoon pure maple syrup
- 2 tablespoons extra-virgin olive oil

Methods (*Servings 4*)

1. Pour the quinoa and vegetable soup in a saucepan. Bring to a boil. Reduce the heat to low. Cover and cook for 15 minutes or until tender. Fluffy with a fork.
2. Meanwhile, combine the ingredients for the mango sauce in a food processor.
3. Pulse until smooth. Divide the quinoa, spinach, and cabbage into 4 serving bowls, then top with chickpeas, avocado, carrots, and bell pepper.
4. Dress them with the mango sauce and spread with cilantro. Serve immediately.

Per serving:

calories: 366 fats: 11.1g protein: 15.5g carbs: 55.6g fiber: 17.7g

Cranberry and Almond Quinoa

Ingredients (*Cook time: 10 minutes*)

- 2 cups water
- 1 cup quinoa, rinsed
- ¼ cup salted sunflower seeds
- ½ cup slivered almonds
- 1 cup dried cranberries

Methods (*Servings 2*)

1. Combine water and quinoa in the Instant Pot. Secure the lid.
2. Select the Manual mode and set the cooking time for 10 minutes at High Pressure.
3. Once cooking is complete, do a quick pressure release.
4. Carefully open the lid. Add sunflower seeds, almonds, and dried cranberries and gently mix until well combined. Serve hot.

Per Serving:

calories: 44 5 fats: 14.8g protein: 15.1g carbs: 64.1g fiber: 10.2g

Chili Halloumi Cheese with Rice

Ingredients (*Cook time: 8 minutes*)

- 2 cups water
- 2 tablespoons brown sugar
- 2 tablespoons rice vinegar
- 1 tablespoon sweet chili sauce
- 1 tablespoon olive oil
- 1 teaspoon fresh minced garlic
- 20 ounces Halloumi cheese, cubed
- 1 cup rice
- ¼ cup chopped fresh chives, for garnish

Methods (*Servings 6*)

1. Heat the oil on Sauté and fry the halloumi for 5 minutes until golden brown. Set aside.
2. To the pot, add water, garlic, olive oil, vinegar, sugar, soy sauce, and chili sauce and mix well until smooth. Stir in rice noodles.
3. Seal the lid and cook on High Pressure for 3 minutes. Release the pressure quickly.

4. Split the rice between bowls. Top with fried halloumi and sprinkle with fresh chives before serving.

Per serving

calories: $34 fats: 34.3g protein: 24.9g carbs: 30.1g fiber: 1.0g

Roasted Butternut Squash and Rice

Ingredients (Cook time: 1$ minutes)

- '/2 cup water
- 2 cups vegetable broth
- 1 small butternut squash, peeled and sliced
- 2 tablespoons olive oil, divided
- 1 teaspoon salt
- 1 teaspoon freshly ground black pepper
- 1 cup feta cheese, cubed
- 1 tablespoon coconut aminos
- 2 teaspoons arrowroot starch
- 1 cup jasmine rice, cooked

Methods (Servings 4)

1. Pour the rice and broth in the pot and stir to combine.
2. In a bowl, toss butternut squash with 1 tablespoon of olive oil and season with salt and black pepper.
3. In another bowl, mix the remaining olive oil, water and coconut aminos.
4. Toss feta in the mixture, add the arrowroot starch, and toss again to combine well. Transfer to a greased baking dish.
5. Lay a trivet over the rice and place the baking dish on the trivet. Seal the lid and cook on High for 15 minutes. Do a quick pressure release, Ouff the rice with a fork and serve with squash an d feta.

calories: 2$8 fats: 14.9g protein: 7.8g carbs: 23.2gJiber: 1.2g

Cumin Quinoa Pilaf

Ingredients (Cook time: $ minutes)

- 2 tablespoons extra virgin olive oil
- 2 cloves garlic, minced
- 3 cups water
- 2 cups quinoa, rinsed
- 2 teaspoons ground cumin
- 2 teaspoons turmeric
- Salt, to taste
- 1 handful parsley, chopped

Methods (Servings 2

1. Press the Sauté button to heat your Instant Po t. Once hot, add the oil and garlic to the pot, stir and cook for 1 minute.
2. Add water, quinoa, cumin, turmeric, and salt, stirring well.
3. Lock the lid. Select the Manual mode and set the cooking time for 1 minute at High Pressure.
4. When the timer beeps, perform a natural pressure release for 10 minutes, then release any remaining pressure.
5. Carefully remove the lid. Fluff the quinoa with a fork. Season with more salt, if needed.
6. Sprinkle the chopped parsley on top and serve.

Per Serving

calories: 384 fats: 12.3g protein: 12.8g carbs: 37.4g fiber: 6.9g

Moroccan-Spiced Chicken Thighs with Saffron Basmati Rice

__Ingredients__ *(Cook time: 15 minutes)*

For the chicken

- ½ teaspoon paprika
- ½ teaspoon cumin
- ½ teaspoon cinnamon
- ¼ teaspoon salt
- ¼ teaspoon garlic powder
- ¼ teaspoon ginger powder
- ¼ teaspoon coriander
- ⅛ teaspoon cayenne pepper
- 10 ounces boneless, skinless chicken thighs (about 4 pieces)

For the rice

- 1 tablespoon olive oil
- ½ small onion, minced
- ½ cup basmati rice
- 2 pinches saffron
- ¼ teaspoon salt
- 1 cup low-sodium chicken stock

__Methods__ *(Servings 2)*

1. To make the chicken. Preheat the oven to 350°F and set the rack to the middle position.
2. In a small bowl, combine the paprika, cumin, cinnamon, salt, garlic powder, ginger powder, coriander, and cayenne pepper. Add chicken thighs and toss, rubbing the spice mix into the chicken.

3. Place the chicken in a baking dish and roast it for 35 to 40 minutes, or until the chicken reaches an internal temperature of 165°F. Let the chicken rest for 5 minutes before serving.

4. To make the rice while the chicken is roasting, heat the oil in a sauté pan over medium-high heat. Add the onion and sauté for 5 minutes.

5. Add the rice, saffron, salt, and chicken stock. Cover the pot with a tight-fitting lid and reduce the heat to low. Let the rice simmer for 15 minutes, or until it is light and Ouffy and the liquid has been absorbed.

Per Serving:

calories: 401; fat: 10g; protein: 3kg carbs: 41g; fiber: 2g

Quick Spanish Rice

Ingredients (Cook time: 1$ minutes)

- 2 tablespoons olive oil
- 1 medium onion, finely chopped
- 1 large tomato, finely diced
- 1 teaspoon smoked paprika
- 2 tablespoons tomato paste
- 1'/2 cups basmati rice
- 1 teaspoon salt
- 3 cups water

Methods (Servings 4)

1. Heat the olive oil in a saucepan over medium heat. Add the onions and tomato and sauté for about 3 minutes until softened.

2. Add the paprika, tomato paste, basmati rice, and salt. Stir the mixture for 1 minute and slowly pour in the water.

3. Reduce the heat to low and allow to simmer covered for 12 minutes, stirring constantly. Remove from the heat and let it rest in the saucepan for 3 minutes.
4. Divide the rice evenly among four serving bowls and serve.
5. For added color and twist, you can sprinkle with freshly chopped cilantro before serving.

Per Serving

Calories: 331 fats: 7.3g protein: 6.1g carbs: 39.8g fiber: 2.1g

Brown Rice Fritters

Ingredients (Cook time: 10 minutes)

- 2 tsps. olive oil
- 1 (10-ounce) bag frozen cooked brown rice, thawed
- 1 egg
- ^{1} cup finely grated carrots
- ^{1} cup minced red bell pepper
- 3 tbsps. brown rice flour
- 3 tbsps. grated Parmesan cheese
- 2 tbsps. minced fresh basil

Methods (Servings 4)

1. Preheat the air fryer to 380°F (193°C).
2. In a small bowl, combine the thawed rice, egg, and Oour and mix to blend. Stir in the carrots, bell pepper, basil, and Parmesan cheese.
3. Form the mixture into 8 fritters and drizzle with the olive oil.
4. Put the fritters carefully into the air fryer basket. Air fry for 8 to 10 minutes, or until the fritters are golden brown and cooked through.
5. Serve immediately.

Per Serving:

Calories: 190, Fat: 6 g, Protein: 7 g, Carbs: 29 g, Fiber: 3 g

Brown Rice and Chili Shrimp Bowl

Ingredients (Cook time: 10-15 minutes)

- 1 tsp. olive oil
- 1 (15-ounce) can seasoned black beans, warmed
- 12 ounces' medium shrimp, peeled and deveined
- 2 cups cooked brown rice
- 1 large avocado, chopped
- 1 cup sliced cherry tomatoes
- 2 tsps. lime juice
- 1 tsp. honey
- 1 tsp. minced garlic
- 1 tsp. chili powder
- Salt, to taste

Methods (Servings 4)

1. Preheat the air fryer to 400°F.
2. Spray the air fryer basket lightly with cooking spray. In a medium bowl, mix together the lime juice, olive oil, honey, garlic, chili powder, and salt to make a marinade.
3. Add the shrimp and toss to coat evenly in the marinade.
4. Place the shrimp in the air fryer basket. Air fry for 5 minutes. Shake the basket and air fry until the shrimp are cooked through and starting to brown, an additional 5 to 10 minutes.
5. To assemble the bowls, spoon ¼ of the rice, black beans, avocado, and cherry tomatoes into each of four bowls.

6. Top with the shrimp and serve.

Per Serving:

Calories: 430, Fat: 1$ g Protein: 28 g Carbs: 49 g Fiber: 13 g

Vegetable Mains

Lemony Roasted Broccoli

Ingredients (Cook time: 15 minutes)

- 2 tsps. extra-virgin olive oil, plus more for coating
- 2 heads broccoli, cut into florets
- 1 clove garlic, minced
- ½ tsp. lemon juice
- 1 tsp. salt
- ½ tsp. black pepper

Methods (Servings 6)

1. Cover the air fryer basket with aluminium foil and coat with a light brushing of oil. Preheat the air fryer to 375ºF (191ºC).
2. In a bowl, combine all ingredients, save for the lemon juice, and transfer to the air fryer basket. Roast for 15 minutes.
3. Serve with the lemon juice.

Per Serving:

Calories: 54, Fat: 2 g, Protein: 3 g, Carbs: 9 g, Fiber: 4 g

Garlicky Mushrooms

Ingredients (Cook time: 10 minutes)

- 1 tbsp. olive oil
- 6 small mushrooms
- 1-ounce onion, peeled and diced
- 1 tbsp. bread crumbs

- 1 tsp. parsley
- 1 tsp. garlic purée
- Salt and ground black pepper, to taste

Methods (Servings 4)

1. Preheat the air fryer to 350°F.
2. Combine the bread crumbs, oil, onion, parsley, salt, pepper and garlic in a bowl.
3. Cut out the mushrooms' stalks and stuff each cap with the crumb mixture.
4. Air fry in the air fryer for 10 minutes.
5. Serve hot.

Per Serving:

Calories: $4, Fat: 4 g Protein: 1 g Carbs: $ g fiber: 1 g

Roasted Eggplant Slices

Ingredients (Cook time: 1$ minutes)

- 2 tbsps. olive oil
- 1 large eggplant, sliced
- '/4 tsp. Salt
- '/2 tsp. garlic powder

Methods (Servings 1)

1. Preheat the air fryer to 390°F.
2. Apply the olive oil to the slices with a brush, coating both sides.
3. Season each side with sprinklings of salt and garlic powder.
4. Put the slices in the air fryer and roast for 15 minutes.
5. Serve immediately.

Per Serving:

Calories: 396, Fat: 28 g, Protein: 5 g, Carbs: 40 g, Fiber: 19 g

Crispy Potatoes

Ingredients (Cook time: 15 minutes)

- 3 tbsps. olive oil
- 6 small potatoes, chopped
- 2 tbsps. fresh parsley, chopped
- 2 tsps. mixed dried herbs
- Salt and black pepper, to taste

Methods (Servings 4)

1. Preheat the Air fryer to 360ºF and grease an Air fryer basket.
2. Mix the potatoes, oil, herbs, salt and black pepper in a bowl.
3. Arrange the chopped potatoes into the Air fryer basket and air fry for about 15 minutes, tossing once in between.
4. Dish out the potatoes onto serving plates and serve garnished with parsley.

Per Serving:

Calories: 232, Fat: 10 g, Protein: 4 g, Carbs: 33 g, Fiber: 4 g

Herbed Carrots

Ingredients (Cook time: 14 minutes)

- 4 tbsps. olive oil
- 6 large carrots, peeled and sliced lengthwise
- ½ cup fat-free Italian dressing
- ½ tbsp. fresh oregano, chopped

- ½ tbsp. fresh parsley, chopped
- Salt and black pepper, to taste

Methods *(Servings 8)*

1. Preheat the Air fryer to 360ºF and grease an Air fryer basket with cooking spray.
2. Mix the carrot slices and 4 tbsps. olive oil in a bowl and toss to coat well.
3. Arrange the carrot slices in the Air fryer basket and air fry for about 12 minutes.
4. Dish out the carrot slices onto serving plates and sprinkle with herbs, salt and black pepper.
5. Transfer into the Air fryer basket and air fry for 2 more minutes. Dish out and serve hot.

Per Serving:

Calories: 90, Fat: 7 g, Protein: 1 g, Carbs: 7 g, Fiber: 2 g

Green Beans and Mushroom Casserole

Ingredients *(Cook time: 12 minutes)*

- 3 tbsps. olive oil
- 24 ounces fresh green beans, trimmed
- 2 cups fresh button mushrooms, sliced
- ⅓ cup French fried onions
- 2 tbsps. fresh lemon juice
- 1 tsp. garlic powder
- 1 tsp. ground sage
- 1 tsp. onion powder Salt and black pepper, to taste

Methods *(Servings 6)*

1. Preheat the Air fryer to 400ºF and grease an Air fryer basket.

2. Mix the green beans, mushrooms, oil, lemon juice, sage, and spices in a bowl and toss to coat well.

3. Arrange the green beans mixture into the Air fryer basket and air fry for about 12 minutes.

4. Dish out in a serving dish and top with fried onions to serve.

Per Serving:

Calories: 120, Fat: 8 g Protein: 3 g Carbs: 11 g fiber: 4 g

Spicy Broccoli Rabe and Artichoke Hearts

Ingredients (Cook time: 1$ minutes)

- 3 tablespoons olive oil, divided
- 2 pounds' fresh broccoli rabe, stems removed and cut into Oorets
- 3 garlic cloves, finely minced
- 1 teaspoon red pepper Oakes
- 1 teaspoon salt, plus more to taste
- 13.5 ounces' artichoke hearts, drained and quartered
- 1 tablespoon water
- 2 tablespoons red wine vinegar
- Freshly ground black pepper, to taste

Methods (Servings 4)

1. Warm 2 tablespoons olive oil in a non-stick skillet over medium-high skillet. Add the broccoli, garlic, red pepper flakes, and salt to the skillet and sauté for 5 minutes or until the broccoli is soft.

2. Add the artichoke hearts to the skillet and sauté for 2 more minutes or until tender.

3. Add water to the skillet and turn down the heat to low. Put the lid on and simmer for 5 minutes.

4. Meanwhile, combine the vinegar and 1 tablespoon of olive oil in a bowl.
5. Drizzle the simmered broccoli and artichokes with oiled vinegar, and sprinkle with salt and black pepper. Toss to combine well before serving.

Per Serving

calories: 272Jats: 21.$g protein: 11.2g carbs: 18.1g fiber: 9.8g

Citrus Pistachios and Asparagus

Ingredients (Cook time: 10 minutes)

- Zest and juice of 2 clementines or 1 orange
- Zest and juice of 1 lemon
- 1 tablespoon red wine vinegar
- 3 tablespoons extra-virgin olive oil, divided
- 1 teaspoon salt, divided
- '/4 teaspoon freshly ground black pepper
- '/2 cup pistachios, shelled
- 1-pound fresh asparagus, trimmed
- 1 tablespoon water

Methods (Servings 4)

1. Combine the zest and juice of clementines and lemon, vinegar, 2 tablespoons of olive oil, 1/2teaspoon of salt, and black pepper in a bowl. Stir to mix well. Set aside.
2. Toast the pistachios in a nonstick skillet over medium-high heat for 2 minutes or until golden brown.
3. Transfer the roasted pistachios to a clean work surface, then chop roughly. Mix the pistachios with the citrus mixture. Set aside.

4. Heat the remaining olive oil in the nonstick skillet over medium-high heat. Add the asparagus to the skillet and sauté for 2 minutes, then season with remaining salt.

5. Add the water to the skillet. Turn down the heat to low, and put the lid on. Simmer for 4 minutes until the asparagus is tender.

6. Remove the asparagus from the skillet to a large dish. Pour the citrus and pistachios mixture over the asparagus. Toss to coat well before serving.

Per Serving

calories: 211 fats: 17.3g protein: 3.9g carbs: 11.2g[ther: 3.8g

Stir-Fried Eggplant

Ingredients (Cook time: 1$ minutes)

- 1 cup water, plus more as needed
- '/2 cup chopped red onion
- 1 tablespoon finely chopped garlic
- 1 tablespoon dried Italian herb seasoning
- 1 teaspoon ground cumin
- 1 small eggplant (about 8 ounces), peeled and cut into $1/2$-inch cubes
- 1 medium carrot, sliced
- 2 cups green beans, cut into 1-inch pieces
- 2 ribs celery, sliced
- 1 cup corn kernels
- 2 tablespoons almond butter
- 2 medium tomatoes, chopped

Methods (Servings 2

1. Heat 1 tablespoon of water in a large soup pot over medium high heat until it sputters.

2. Cook the onion for 2 minutes, adding a little more water as needed.
3. Add the garlic, Italian seasoning, cumin, an d eggplant and stir-fry for 2 to 3 minutes, adding a little more water as needed.
4. Add the carrot, green beans, celery, corn kernels, and $1/2$ cup of water and stir well. Reduce the heat to medium, cover, and cook for 8 to 10 minutes, stirring occasionally, or until the vegetables are tender.
5. Meanwhile, in a bowl, stir together the almond butter and $1/2$ cup of water.
6. Remove the vegetables from the heat and stir in the almond butter mixture and chopped tomatoes. Cool for a few minutes before serving.

Per Servings

calories: 176 fats: $.$g protein: 3.8g carbs: 25.4gJiber: 8.6g

Tradicional Matchuba Green Beans

Ingredients (Cook time: 1$ minutes)

- 1 $1/4$lb narrow green beans, trimmed
- 3 tbsp butter, melted
- 1 cup Moroccan matbucha
- 2 green onions, chopped
- Salt and black pepper to taste

Methods (Servings 4)

1. Steam the green beans in a pot for 5-6 minutes until tender.
2. Remove to a bowl, reserving the cooking liquid.
3. In a skillet over medium heat, melt the butter.
4. Add in green onions, salt, and black pepper and cook until fragrant.
5. Lower the heat and put in the green beans along with some of the reserved water.

6. Simmer for 3-4 minutes. Serve the green beans with the Sabra Moroccan matbucha as a dip.

Per Serving:

Calories: 125; Fat: 8.6g; Protein: 2.2g; Carbs: 9g.

Cauliflower with Sweet Potato

Ingredients (Cook time: 8 minutes)

- 1 small onion
- 4 tomatoes
- 4 garlic cloves, chopped
- 2-inch ginger, chopped
- 2 teaspoons olive oil
- 1 teaspoon turmeric
- 2 teaspoons ground cumin
- Salt, to taste
- 1 teaspoon paprika
- 2 medium sweet potatoes, cubed small
- 2 small cauliflowers, diced
- 2 tablespoons fresh chopped cilantro for topping

Methods (Servings 8)

1. Blend the tomatoes, garlic, ginger and onion in a blender. Add the oil and cumin in the instant pot and Sauté for 1 minute.
2. Stir in the blended mixture and the remaining spices. Add the sweet potatoes and cook for 5 minutes on Sauté
3. Add the cauliflower chunks and secure the lid. Cook on Manual for 2 minutes at High Pressure.
4. Once done, Quick release the pressure and remove the lid.

5. Stir and serve with cilantro on top.

Per Serving:

calories: 76 fats: 1.6g protein: 2.7g carbs: 14.4g fiber: 3.4g

Simple Oven-baked Green Beans

Ingredients *(Cook time: 15 minutes)*

- 2 tbsp. olive oil
- 2 lb green beans, trimmed
- Salt and black pepper to taste

Methods *(Servings 6)*

1. Preheat oven to 400 F.
2. Toss the green beans with some olive oil, salt, and spread them in a single layer on a greased baking dish.
3. Roast for 8-10 minutes.
4. Transfer green beans to a serving platter and drizzle with the remaining olive oil.

Per Serving:

calories: 157; fat: 2g; protein: 3g; carbs: 6g.

Ratatouille

Ingredients *(Cook time: 6 minutes)*

- 2 large zucchinis, sliced
- 2 medium eggplants, sliced
- 4 medium tomatoes, sliced

- 2 small red onions, sliced
- 4 cloves garlic, chopped
- 2 tablespoons thyme leaves
- 2 cups gluten-free rolled oats
- ½ cup raisins
- ¾ cup chopped pecans
- ¼ teaspoon ground nutmeg
- 1 teaspoon ground cinnamon
- ½ teaspoon ground ginger
- ¼ teaspoon sea salt

Methods *(Servings 4)*

1. Line a spring form pan with foil and place the chopped garlic in the bottom.
2. Now arrange the vegetable slices, alternately, in circles.
3. Sprinkle the thyme, pepper and salt over the vegetables.
4. Top with oil and vinegar. Pour a cup of water into the instant pot and places the trivet inside.
5. Secure the lid and cook on Manual function for 6 minutes at High Pressure.
6. Release the pressure naturally and remove the lid. Remove the vegetables along with the tin foil. Serve on a platter and enjoy.

Per Serving:

calories: 240 fats: 14.3g protein: 4.7g carbs: 27.5g | fiber: 10.8g

Parmesan Stuffed Zucchini Boats

Ingredients *(Cook time: 15 minutes)*

- 1 cup canned low-sodium chickpeas, drained and rinsed
- 1 cup no-sugar-added spaghetti sauce
- 2 zucchinis

- ¼ cup shredded Parmesan cheese

Methods *(Servings 4)*

1. Preheat the oven to 425ºF. In a medium bowl, stir together the chickpeas and spaghetti sauce.
2. Cut the zucchini in half lengthwise and scrape a spoon gently down the length of each half to remove the seeds.
3. Fill each zucchini half with the chickpea sauce and top with one-quarter of the Parmesan cheese.
4. Place the zucchini halves on a baking sheet and roast in the oven for 15 minutes.
5. Transfer to a plate. Let rest for 5 minutes before serving.

Per Serving:

calories: 139; fat: 4.0g; protein: 8.0g; carbs: 20.0g.

Sweet Potato and Tomato Curry

Ingredients *(Cook time: 8 minutes)*

- 2 large brown onions, finely diced
- 4 tablespoons olive oil
- 4 teaspoons salt
- 4 large garlic cloves, diced
- 1 red chili, sliced
- 4 tablespoons cilantro, chopped
- 4 teaspoons ground cumin
- 2 teaspoons ground coriander
- 2 teaspoons paprika
- 2 pounds' sweet potato, diced
- 4 cups chopped, tinned tomatoes
- 2 cups water

- 2 cups vegetable stock
- Lemon juice and cilantro (garnish)

Methods (Servings 8)

1. Put the oil and onions into the instant pot an d Sauté for 5 minutes.
2. Stir in the remaining ingredients and secure the lid.
3. Cook on Manual function for 3 minutes at High Pressure.
4. Once done, Quick release the pressure and remove the lid.
5. Garnish with cilantro and lemon juice. Serve.

Per Serving:

calories: 224 fats: 8.0g protein: 4.6g carbs: 35.9gJiber: 7.$g

Grilled Vegetable Skewers

Ingredients (Cook time: 10 minutes)

- 4 medium red onions, peeled and sliced into 6 wedges
- 4 medium zucchini, cut into 1-inch-thick slices
- 2 beefsteak tomatoes, cut into quarters
- 4 red bell peppers, cut into 2-inch squares
- 2 orange bell peppers, cut into 2-inch squares
- 2 yellow bell peppers, cut into 2-inch squares
- 2 tablespoons plus 1 teaspoon olive oil, divided

Methods (Servings 4)

1. Preheat the grill to medium-high heat.
2. Skewer the vegetables by alternating between red onion, zucchini, tomatoes, and the different colored bell peppers.
3. Brush them with 2 tablespoons of olive oil.

4. Rub oil on the grill grates with 1 teaspoon of olive oil and grill the vegetable skewers for 5 minutes.
5. Flip the skewers and grill for 5 minutes more, or until they are cooked to your liking.
6. Let the skewers cool for 5 minutes before serving.

Per Serving:

calories: 115; fat: 3.0g; protein: 3.5g; carbs: 18.7g.

Butternut Noodles with Mushrooms

Ingredients (*Cook time: 12 minutes*)

- ¼ cup extra-virgin olive oil
- 1 pound cremini mushrooms, sliced
- ½ red onion, finely chopped
- 1 teaspoon dried thyme
- ½ teaspoon sea salt
- 3 garlic cloves, minced
- ½ cup dry white wine
- Pinch of red pepper flakes
- 4 cups butternut noodles
- 4 ounces grated Parmesan cheese

Methods (*Servings 4*)

1. In a large skillet over medium-high h eat, heat the olive oil until shimmering.
2. Add the mushrooms, onion, thyme, and salt to the skillet. Cook for about 6 minutes, stirring occasionally, or until the mushrooms star t to brown.
3. Add the garlic and sauté for 30 seconds. Stir in the white wine and red pepper flakes.

4. Fold in the noodles. Cook for about 5 minutes, stirring occasionally, or until the noodles are tender.
5. Serve topped with the grated Parmesan.

Per Serving:

calories: 244 fat: 14.0g *protein: 4.0g carbs: 22.0g fiber: 4.0g*

Honey-Glazed Baby Carrots

Ingredients (Cook time: 6 minutes)

- ² cup water
- 1'/2 pounds baby carrots
- 4 tablespoons almond butter
- '/2 cup honey
- 1 teaspoon dried thyme
- 1'/2 teaspoons dried dill Salt, to taste

Methods (Servings 2

1. Pour the water into the Instant Pot and add a steamer basket.
2. Place the baby carrots in the basket. Secure the lid. Select the Manual mode and set the cooking time for 4 minutes at High Pressure.
3. Once cooking is complete, do a quick pressure release. Carefully open the lid. Transfer the carrots to a plate and set aside.
4. Pour the water out of the Instant Pot and dry it. Press the Sauté button on the Instant Pot and heat the almond butter. Stir in the honey, thyme, and dill.
5. Return the carrots to the Instant Pot and stir until well coated. Sauté for another 1 minute.
6. Taste and season with salt as needed. Serve warm.

Per Serving:

calories: 575 fats: 23.5g protein: 2.8g carbs: 90.6g fiber: 10.3g

Cauliflower Hash with Carrots

Ingredients (Cook time: 10 minutes)

- 3 tablespoons extra-virgin olive oil
- 1 large onion, chopped
- 1 tablespoon minced garlic
- 2 cups diced carrots
- 4 cups cauliflower florets
- ½ teaspoon ground cumin
- 1 teaspoon salt

Methods (Servings 4)

1. In a large skillet, heat the olive oil over medium heat.
2. Add the onion and garlic and saut é for 1 minute. Stir in the carrots and stir-fry for 3 minutes.
3. Add the cauliflower florets, cumin, an d salt and toss to combine.
4. Cover and cook for 3 minutes until lightly br owned. Stir well and cook, uncovered, for 3 to 4 minutes, until softened.
5. Remove from the heat and serve warm.

Per Serving:

calories: 158 fats: 10.8g protein: 3.1g carbs: 14.9g fiber: 5.1g

Soups

White Bean Soup and Gremolata

Ingredients (*Cook time: 15 minutes*)

For the soup:

- 2 teaspoons olive oil
- 2 teaspoons garlic, minced
- 2 cups chicken broth, fat-free, less-sodium
- 2 cans (19-ounce each) cannellini beans, rinsed, drained
- 1/4 teaspoon black pepper
- 1/2 cup water
- 1/2 cup pancetta, finely chopped
- 1/2 cup celery, pre-chopped
- 1 cup onion, pre-chopped
- 1 bay leaf

For the gremolata:

- 2 teaspoons lemon rind, freshly grated
- 1 tablespoon fresh parsley, chopped
- 1 teaspoon garlic, minced

Methods (*Servings 4*)

1. For the soup: In a large-sized saucepan, heat the oil over medium-high heat. Add the pancetta and cook for 2 minutes.
2. Stir in the onion, the celery, and the garlic; sauté for about 3 minutes or until almost tender.
3. Stir in the broth, the water, black pepper, the beans, and the bay leaf; bring the mixture to a boil. Reduce the heat; simmer, stirring occasionally, for 8 minutes.
4. For the gremolata: Combine all of the ingredients; sprinkle over the soup.

calories 227, fat 7.6 g protein 9.8 g carb 28.7 g fiber 7.7 g

Prosciutto and Pea Soup

Ingredients (Cook time: 1$ minutes)

- 4 cups frozen peas
- 3 tablespoons olive oil
- 2 vegetable stock cubes
- 2 garlic cloves, crushed
- 1/2 cup light sour cream
- 1/5 lb. prosciutto
- 5 cups water
- 1 leek, trimmed, halved lengthways, and thinly sliced

Methods (Servings 6)

1. In a frying pan, heat 1 tablespoon of the olive oil over medium-high heat. Add 1/2 of the prosciutto; cook for 1 minute per side or until crispy; transfer to a plate, break into large pieces, and reserve.
2. In a large saucepan, heat the remaining olive oil over medium heat.
3. Coarsely chop the remaining prosciutto; add to the pan. Add the garlic and leek; cook, for 3 minutes, stirring, or until soft.
4. Add the water and the vegetable stock cubes; bring to a boil. Add the peas; cook for 5 minutes, stirring occasionally, or until just cooked. Set aside and let cool slightly for 5 minutes.
5. Pour 1/3 of the pea mixture in a blender and process until smooth; transfer into a clean saucepan. Repeat the process with the remaining mixture, blending in 2 batches. Over medium heat, heat for 2 minutes or until heated through; season with the salt and pepper.

6. Divide the soup between serving bowls; top with the sour cream and the reserved prosciutto. Serve with garlic bread.

Per Serving:

calories 366.2., [at 26 g protein 13 g, carb 17 g., fiber 7 g

Chunky fish soup

Ingredients (Cook time: 10 minutes)

- 1 bulb fennel, finely sliced
- 1 teaspoon chipotle chili in chili paste or adobo sauce, to serve
- 2 courgette (zucchini), finely sliced
- 2 cups fish stock
- 1 Ib. hoki fillet, defrosted, cut into 4-inch pieces
- 5 tablespoons half-fat creme fraiche, to serve
- 1 Ib. tub Napolitano pasta sauce (tomato and basil)
- Handful fresh basil, torn

Methods (Servings 4)

1. Pour the stock and the pasta sauce into a large-sized saucepan; bring to a boil and simmer 2 to 3 minutes. Add the courgette and the fennel; simmer for 2 minutes.
2. Add the hoki cubes into the soup; poach for 2-3 minutes over low heat or until the fish is cooked.
3. Do not stir often or the fish will break. Gently stir in the basil; adjust the seasoning.
4. In a bowl, mix in the chipotle chili and the creme fraiche; season.
5. Ladle the soups into bowl, spoon a dollop of the creme fraiche mixture on top, and serve.

Per Serving:

calories 164., fat 4 g, (1 g sat. fat), protein 23 g, carb 9 g, fiber 3 g

Creamy Tomato Hummus Soup

Ingredients *(Cook time: 10 minutes)*

- 1 (14.5-ounce) can crushed tomatoes with basil
- 1 cup roasted red pepper hummus
- 2 cups low-sodium chicken stock Salt
- ¼ cup fresh basil leaves, thinly sliced (optional, for garnish)
- Garlic croutons (optional, for garnish)

Methods *(Servings 2)*

1. Combine the canned tomatoes, hummus, and chicken stock in a blender and blend until smooth.
2. Pour the mixture into a saucepan and bring it to a boil.
3. Season with salt and fresh basil if desired.
4. Serve with garlic croutons as a garnish, if desired.

Per Serving:

Calories: 148; fat: 6g; Protein: 5g; carbs: 19g; Fiber: 4g.

Beef Stew with Tomato and Lentil

Ingredients: (Cook time: 10 minutes)

- 2 tbsps. extra-virgin olive oil
- 1 onion, chopped

- 1-pound extra-lean ground beef
- 1 (14-ounce,) can chopped tomatoes with garlic and basil, drained
- 1 (14-ounce) can lentils, drained
- ½ tsp. sea salt
- ⅛ tsp. freshly ground black pepper

Methods: (Servings: 4)

1. Heat the olive oil in a large pot over medium-high heat, until it shimmers.
2. Stir in the onion and beef. Cook for about 5 minutes, use a wooden spoon to crumble the beef until it browns.
3. Add the tomatoes, lentils, salt and pepper, stir well and bring to a simmer.
4. Lower the heat to medium. Cook and stir until the lentils are hot, about 3 to 4 minutes.

Per Serving:

Calories: 461, Fat: 15 g, Protein: 44 g, Carbs: 37 g

Peas and Orzo Soup

Ingredients (Cook time: 10 minutes)

- ½ cup orzo
- 6 cups chicken soup
- 1 and ½ cups cheddar, shredded
- Salt and black pepper to the taste
- 2 teaspoons oregano, dried
- ¼ cup yellow onion, chopped
- 3 cups baby spinach
- 2 tablespoons lime juice
- ½ cup peas

Methods (*Servings 4*)

1. Heat up a pot with the soup over medium heat, add the orzo and the rest of the ingredients except the cheese.
2. Bring to a simmer and cook for 10 minutes.
3. Add the cheese, stir, divide into bowls and serve.

Per Serving:

calories 360, fat 10.2, protein 22.3, carbs 43.3, fiber 4.7

Authentic Gazpacho Soup

Ingredients (*Cook time: 0 minutes*)

- ½ cup of water
- 2 slices of whole-grain bread, crust removed
- 1 Persian cucumber, peeled and chopped
- 2 pounds' ripe tomatoes
- 1 clove garlic, finely chopped
- $\frac{1}{3}$ cup extra-virgin olive oil, plus more for serving
- 2 tablespoons red wine vinegar
- 1 teaspoon salt
- ½ teaspoon freshly ground black pepper

Methods (*Servings 6-8*)

1. Soak the bread in a bowl of water for about 5 minutes, then discard the water.
2. In a food processor, put the bread, cucumber, tomatoes, garlic, olive oil, red wine vinegar, salt, and pepper.
3. Process the ingredients until completely mixed and glossy.
4. Pour the mixture into a glass jar and refrigerate to chill until ready to serve. To serve, drizzle the soup with olive oil.

5. You can top the soup with fresh herbs of your choice, such as thyme, basil or parsley. For added crispness and sweetness, you can add ½ red onion.

Per Serving:

Calories: 165 fats: 13.3g protein: 2.2g carbs: 12.2g fiber: 2.1g

Mediterranean Tomato Hummus Soup

Ingredients *(Cook time: 10 minutes)*

- 1 can crushed tomatoes with basil
- 2 cups low-sodium chicken stock
- 1 cup roasted red pepper hummus
- Salt, to taste
- ¼ cup thinly sliced fresh basil leaves, for garnish (optional)

Methods *(Servings 2)*

1. Combine the canned tomatoes, hummus, and chicken stock in a blender and blend until smooth.
2. Pour the mixture into a saucepan and bring it to a boil.
3. Season with salt to taste.
4. Serve garnished with the fresh basil, if desired.

Per Serving:

calories: 147; fat: 6.2g; protein: 5.2g; carbs: 20.1g.

Chicken and Orzo Soup

Ingredients *(Cook time: 11 minutes)*

- ½ cup carrot, chopped
- 1 yellow onion, chopped
- 12 cups chicken stock
- 2 cups kale, chopped
- 3 cups chicken meat, cooked and shredded
- 1 cup orzo
- ¼ cup lemon juice
- 1 tablespoon olive oil

Methods (*Servings 4*)

1. Heat up a pot with the oil over medium heat, add the onion and sauté for 3 minutes.
2. Add the carrots and the rest of the ingredients, stir, bring to a simmer and cook for 8 minutes more.
3. Ladle into bowls and serve hot.

Per Serving:

calories 300, fat 12.2, protein 12.2, carbs 16.5, fiber 5.4.

Tuscan Soup

Ingredients (*Cook time: 15 minutes*)

- 1 yellow onion, chopped
- 4 garlic cloves, minced
- 2 tablespoons olive oil
- ½ cup celery, chopped
- ½ cup carrots, chopped
- 15 ounces canned tomatoes, chopped
- 1 zucchini, chopped
- 6 cups veggie stock

- 2 tablespoons tomato paste
- 15 ounces canned white beans, drained and rinsed
- 2 handfuls baby spinach
- 1 tablespoon basil, chopped
- Salt and black pepper to the taste

Methods (Servings 6)

1. Heat up a pot with the oil over medium heat, add the garlic and the onion and sauté for 5 minutes.
2. Add the rest of the ingredients, stir, bring the soup to a simmer and cook for 10 minutes.
3. Ladle the soup into bowls and serve right away.

Per Serving:

calories 471, fat 8.2, protein 27.6, carbs 76.5, fiber 19.4.

Kale and White Bean Soup

Ingredients: (Cook time: 13 minutes)

- 3 tbsps. olive oil
- 1 (28 oz) can diced tomatoes
- 4 cups kale 1 white onion, chopped
- 30 oz. white cannellini beans
- 4 cups vegetable stock

Methods: (Servings: 10)

1. Set the Instant Pot to Sauté and heat the olive oil. Sauté the white onion for 3 minutes, stirring occasionally.
2. Add the tomatoes, beans, and vegetable stock, and whisk well. Lock the lid.
3. Select the Manual mode, then set the timer for 10 minutes at High Pressure.

4. Once the timer goes off, do a quick pressure release. Carefully open the lid. Stir in the kale.
5. Cover the pot and let rest for a few minutes until the kale is wilted. Serve warm.

Per Serving:

Calories 240; fat: 8g; Protein: 10g. Carbs: 34g

Peas Soup

Ingredients (Cook time: 10 minutes)

- 1 white onion, chopped
- 1 tablespoon olive oil
- 1-quart veggie stock
- 2 eggs
- 3 tablespoons lemon juice
- 2 cups peas
- 2 tablespoons parmesan, grated
- Salt and black pepper to the taste

Methods (Servings 4)

1. Heat up a pot with the oil over medium-high heat, add the onion and sauté for 4 minutes.
2. Add the rest of the ingredients except the eggs, bring to a simmer and cook for 4 minutes.
3. Add whisked eggs, stir the soup, cook for 2 minutes more, divide into bowls and serve.

Per Serving:

calories 293, fat 11.2 protein 4.43, carbs 27, fiber 3.4

Mediterranean-Style Turkey Chili

Ingredients *(Cook time: 13 minutes)*

- 1 large onion, chopped
- 1-pound ground turkey, 93% lean
- 1 red chili pepper, seeded, finely chopped
- 1 tablespoons tomato paste
- 1-2 cloves garlic, finely chopped
- 2 cans (14 ounces each) diced tomatoes
- 2 cans (15 ounces each) white beans, drained and rinsed
- 2 cups chicken stock
- 3 ounces IRlamata olives
- 3 ounces sun-dried tomatoes, thinly sliced
- 3 tablespoons olive oil
- 4 ounces' arugula leaves
- 4 ounces' feta cheese, crumbled

Methods *(Servings 4)*

1. Through a sieve, strain the tomatoes; reserve the juice. In a Dutch oven, heat the oil over medium-high heat.
2. Add the turkey; sauté until crumbly. Add the garlic, onion, and chili pepper; sauté for 2 to 3 minutes.
3. Stir in the tomato paste. Add the stock, the sundried tomatoes, and the tomato juice; bring the mixture to a boil.
4. Reduce the heat to medium-low, cover, and simmer for 5 minutes. Add the beans, canned tomatoes, and olives.
5. Cook for 5 minutes more and season with the chili. Serve garnished with crumbled feta and arugula.

Chili Watermelon Soup

Ingredients (*Cook time: 0 minutes*)

- 2 pounds' watermelon, peeled and cubed
- ½ teaspoon chipotle chili powder
- 2 tablespoons olive oil
- A pinch of salt and white pepper
- 1 tomato, chopped
- 1 shallot, chopped
- ¼ cup cilantro, chopped
- 1 small cucumber, chopped
- 2 tablespoons lemon juice
- ½ tablespoon red wine vinegar

Methods (*Servings 4*)

1. In a blender, combine the watermelon with the chili powder, the oil and the rest of the ingredients except the vinegar and the lemon juice, pulse well, and divide into bowls.
2. Top each serving with lemon juice and vinegar and serve.

Per Servings:

calories 120, fat 4.5, protein 2.3, carbs 12, fiber 3.4

Mediterranean-Style Vegetable Stew

Ingredients (Cook time: 15 minutes)

- 1 can (14 ounces) cannelini beans, rinsed, drained
- 1 red onion, peeled, chopped
- 1 tablespoon cilantro, chopped
- 2 cloves garlic, peeled, crushed
- 2 small zucchinis, thinly sliced
- 2 tablespoons lemon juice
- 2 tablespoons olive oil, divided
- 3 tomatoes, quartered
- 4 cups vegetable stock
- 5 ounces' carrots, peeled, cut into ribbons using a vegetable peeler
- 8 ounces' turnips, peeled, chopped
- Crusty whole-wheat bread, to serve
- Lemon wedges, to serve

Methods (Servings 4)

1. In a large-sized pot, heat 1 tablespoons of the olive oil. Add the garlic, onion, and turnip; sauté for 5 minutes. Add the carrots, tomatoes, zucchini; sauté for 2 minutes.
2. Add the stock, the lemon juice, the beans, and the remaining oil; season to taste. Bring to a boil; simmer for 3 to 4 minutes.
3. Sprinkle with cilantro. Serve with the bread and the lemon wedges.

Per Serving:

Calories 190, fat 11 g, protein 5 g, carb 29 g, fiber 9 g.

Shrimp Soup

Ingredients (*Cook time: 5 minutes*)

- 1 cucumber, chopped
- 3 cups tomato juice
- 3 roasted red peppers, chopped
- 3 tablespoons olive oil
- 2 tablespoons balsamic vinegar
- 1 garlic clove, minced
- Salt and black pepper to the taste
- ½ teaspoon cumin, ground
- 1 pound's shrimp, peeled and deveined
- 1 teaspoon thyme, chopped

Methods (*Servings 6*)

1. In your blender, mix cucumber with tomato juice, red peppers, 2 tablespoons oil, the vinegar, cumin, salt, pepper and the garlic, pulse well.
2. Transfer to a bowl and keep in the fridge for 10 minutes.
3. Heat up a pot with the rest of the oil over medium heat, add the shrimp, salt, pepper and the thyme and cook for 2 minutes on each side.
4. Divide cold soup into bowls, top with the shrimp and serve.

Per Serving:

calories 263, fat 11.1, protein 6.32, carbs 12.5, fiber 2.4

Creamy Salmon Soup

Ingredients (*Cook time: 15 minutes*)

- 2 tablespoons olive oil

- 1 red onion, chopped
- Salt and white pepper to the taste
- 3 gold potatoes, peeled and cubed
- 2 carrots, chopped
- 4 cups fish stock
- 4 ounces' salmon fillets, boneless and cubed
- ½ cup heavy cream
- 1 tablespoon dill, chopped

Methods *(Servings 6)*

1. Heat up a pan with the oil over medium heat, add the onion, and sauté for 5 minutes.
2. Add the rest of the ingredients expect the cream, salmon and the dill, bring to a simmer and cook for 5-6 minutes more.
3. Add the salmon, cream and the dill, simmer for 5 minutes more, divide into bowls.
4. Serve and enjoy.

Per Serving:

calories 214, fat 16.3, protein 11.8, carbs 6.4, fiber 1.5.

Grapes, Cucumbers and Almonds Soup

Ingredients *(Cook time: 0 minutes)*

- ¼ cup almonds, chopped and toasted
- 3 cucumbers, peeled and chopped
- 3 garlic cloves, minced
- ½ cup warm water
- 6 scallions, sliced
- ¼ cup white wine vinegar

- 3 tablespoons olive oil
- Salt and white pepper to the taste
- 1 teaspoon lemon juice
- ½ cup green grapes, halved

Methods (*Servings 4*)

1. In your blender, combine the almonds with the cucumbers and the rest of the ingredients except the grapes and lemon juice, pulse well and divide into bowls.
2. Top each serving with the lemon juice and grapes and serve cold.

Per Serving:

calories 200, fat 5.4, protein 3.3, carbs 7.6, fiber 2.4.

Spinach and Orzo Soup

Ingredients: (*Cook time: 10 minutes*)

- ½ cup orzo
- 6 cups chicken soup
- 1 and ½ cups parmesan, grated
- Salt and black pepper to taste
- 1 and ½ tsp. oregano, dried
- ¼ cup yellow onion, finely chopped
- 3 cups baby spinach
- 2 tbsp. lemon juice
- ½ cup peas, frozen

Methods: (*Servings: 4*):

1. Heat a saucepan with the stock over high heat.
2. Add oregano, orzo, onion, salt and pepper, stir, bring to a boil, cover and cook for 10 minutes.

3. Take soup off the heat, add salt and pepper to taste and the rest of the ingredients, stir well and divide into soup bowls.
4. Serve right away.

Per Serving:

Calories 201, Fat 5g, Protein 17g, Carbs 28g

Fish and Sea Food

Garlic-Lemon Tilapia

Ingredients: (Cook time: 15 minutes)

- 1 tbsp. lemon juice
- 1 tbsp. olive oil
- 1 tsp. minced garlic
- ½ tsp. chili powder
- 4 (6-ounce) tilapia fillets

Methods: (Servings: 4):

1. Preheat the air fryer to 380ºF (193ºC). Line the air fryer basket with parchment paper.
2. In a large, shallow bowl, mix together the lemon juice, olive oil, garlic, and chili powder to make a marinade. Place the tilapia fillets in the bowl and coat evenly.
3. Place the fillets in the basket in a single layer, leaving space between each fillet.
4. You may need to cook in more than one batch.
5. Air fry until the fish is cooked and flakes easily with a fork, 10 to 15 minutes. Serve hot.

Per Serving:

calories: 183, fat: 5 g, protein: 32 g, carbs: 1 g

Very-Berry Sweet Chili Salmon Fillets

Ingredients: (Cook time: 15 minutes)

- 2 tbsp. sweet chili sauce (divided)
- 1 spring onion, finely chopped

- 1 Persian cucumber, finely chopped
- 1 cup fresh blackberries
- 1 tbsp. avocado oil
- 4 skin-on salmon fillets
- 1/2 tsp. Oaky sea salt
- 1/2 tsp. freshly ground black pepper

Methods• (Servings: 4):

1. In a bowl, gently stir together 1 tablespoon of sweet chili sauce and the spring onion, cucumber, and blackberries. Set aside.
2. Preheat a grill to medium-high heat with 1 tablespoon of oil. Season the salmon fillets with salt and pepper before placing them skin down on the heated grill.
3. Place a lid on the grill, and cook the fillets for 2-3 minutes before brushing them with the remaining chili sauce.
4. Replace the lid. Continue to cook for 10-12 minutes or until the fillets are opaque.
5. Serve the cooked salmon hot, topped with the blackberry mixture.

Per Serving:

calories: 303 fats: 16g protein: 30g carbs: 9g

Healthy Tuna & Bean Wraps

Ingredients: (Cook time: 0 minutes)

- 15 oz. canned cannellini beans drained and rinsed
- 12 oz. canned (drained and flaked) light tuna in water
- 1/8 tsp. white pepper 1/8 tsp. kosher salt
- 1 tbsp. fresh parsley, chopped
- 2 tbsp. extra-virgin avocado oil
- '/4 cup red onion, chopped

- 12 romaine lettuce leaves
- 1 medium-sized ripe
- Hass avocado, sliced

Methods: *(Servings: 4)*

1. In a bowl, stir the beans, tuna, pepper, salt, parsley, avocado oil, and red onions.
2. Spoon some of the mixture onto each lettuce leaf.
3. Top with the sliced avocado before folding and serving.

Per Serving:

calories: 279 fats: 13g carbs: 19g protein: 22g

Olive Baked Cod Fillets

Ingredients: *(Cook time: 15 minutes)*

- 4 cod fillets
- 2 tbsp. extra-virgin avocado oil
- 1/4 tsp. kosher salt
- 1/8 tsp. white pepper
- 1/2 small shallot, thinly sliced
- 1 small green pepper, thinly sliced
- 1/4 cup (pitted and chopped) olives
- 8 oz. canned tomato sauce
- 1/4 cup mozzarella cheese, grated

Methods: *(Servings: 4)*

1. Set the oven to preheat to 400F, with the wire rack in the center of the oven.
2. Coat a casserole dish with baking spray. Arrange the cod fillets in the prepared casserole dish. Use a basting brush to coat the fillets with the oil, and season with salt and pepper.

3. Top the seasoned fillets with the shallots, green peppers, and olives. Pour the tomato sauce over everything in the dish, and top with the cheese.

4. Bake in the oven for 15 minutes, or until the fish is flaky and opaque.

Per Serving:

calories: 246 fats: 12g carbs: 6g protein: 29g

Two-Way Tilapia Fillets

Ingredients: (Cook time: 1$ minutes)

- 6 tilapia fillets
- 2 cups diced tomatoes
- 1 tsp. crushed oregano
- 1 tsp. crushed sweet basil
- 2 tsp. crushed garlic Oakes
- '/2 cup roasted sweet peppers, chopped
- '/4 cup button mushrooms, sliced
- '/2 cup mozzarella, grated
- '/2 cup (pitted and diced) I(alamata olives
- 1 whole avocado, sliced '/2 cup frozen corn (thawed)
- '/2 cup feta cheese, crumbled
- 1 tsp. fresh coriander leaves, chopped

Methods• (Servings: 6)

1. Set the oven to preheat to 400F, with the wire rack in the center of the oven. Coat a baking tray with cooking spray.

2. Place the tilapia fillets on the prepared baking sheet, 3 per side. Divide the crushed tomatoes between the 6 fillets.

3. Top 3 of the fillets with oregano, sweet basil, crushed garlic, roasted sweet peppers, mushrooms, and mozzarella.

4. Top each of the remaining fillets with the olives, avocado, corn, feta, and fresh coriander.
5. Bake the tilapia in the oven for 15 minutes. Serve hot.

Per Serving:

calories: 197 fats: 4g protein: 34g carbs: 5g

Zesty Scallops & Pasta

Ingredients: (Cook time: 10-15 minutes)

- 4 oz. raw fettuccine
- 1 tbsp. extra-virgin avocado oil
- 1/4 tsp. cayenne pepper
- 1/2 tsp. lemon zest, finely grated
- 1 tsp. crushed garlic
- 1/2 medium sweet red pepper, julienned
- 1 tbsp. freshly squeezed lemon juice
- 1/4 cup white wine
- 1/2 cup low-sodium chicken stock 6 sea scallops
- 2 tsp. parmesan cheese, grated

Methods: (Servings: 2)

1. Prepare the fettuccine according to the instructions on the packaging, and set it aside. While the pasta cooks, heat the oil in a pan.
2. Add the cayenne pepper, lemon zest, garlic, and sweet red pepper, and fry for 2 minutes.
3. Whisk in the white wine, lemon juice, and chicken stock. When the stock begins to boil, lower the heat, and simmer uncovered for 5-6 minutes, or until half of the liquid has evaporated.

4. Half the scallops horizontally before adding them to the simmering sauce. Cover for 4-5 minutes. Stir occasionally.
5. Serve the cooked scallops and sauce on a bed of cooked fettuccine, and garnish with the parmesan before serving.

Per Serving:

Calories: 421 fat: 10g Protein: 30g Carbs: 49g

Glazed Broiled Salmon

Ingredients: (Cook time: $-10 minutes)

- 4 (4-ounce/ 113-g) salmon fillets
- 3 tablespoons miso paste
- 2 tablespoons raw honey
- 1 teaspoon coconut aminos
- 1 teaspoon rice vinegar

Methods• (Servings: 4)

1. Preheat the broiler to High. Lin e a baking dish with aluminum foil and add the salmon fillets.
2. Whisk together the miso paste, honey, coconut aminos, and vinegar in a small bowl. Pour the glaze over the fillets and spread it evenly with a brush.
3. Broil for about 5 minutes, or until the salmon is browned on top and opaque. Brush any remaining glaze over the salmon and broil for an additional 5 minutes if needed.
4. Let the salmon cool for 5 minutes before serving.

Per Serving:

calories: 263 fats: 8.9g protein: 30.2g carbs: 12.8g fiber: 0.7g

Fried Cod Fillets

Ingredients: (Cook time: 10 minutes)

- ½ cup all-purpose flour
- 1 teaspoon garlic powder
- 1 teaspoon salt
- 4 (4- to 5-ounce) cod fillets
- 1 tablespoon extra-virgin olive oil

Methods: (Servings: 4)

1. Mix together the flour, garlic powder, and salt in a shallow dish. Dredge each piece of fish in the seasoned flour until they are evenly coated.
2. Heat the olive oil in a medium skillet over medium-high h eat.
3. Once hot, add the cod fillets and fry for 6 to 8 minutes, flipping the fish half way through, or until the fish is opaque and flakes easily.
4. Remove from the heat and serve on plates.

Per Serving:

calories: 333 fats: 18.8g protein: 21.2g carbs: 20.0g fiber: 5.7g

Breaded Shrimp

Ingredients: (Cook time: 4-6 minutes)

- 2 large eggs
- 1 tablespoon water
- 2 cups seasoned Italian bread crumbs
- 1 teaspoon salt

- 1 cup flour
- 1-pound large shrimp (21 to 25), peeled and deveined
- Extra-virgin olive oil, as needed

Methods• *(Servings: 4)*

1. In a small bowl, beat the eggs with the water, then transfer to a shallow dish. Add the bread crumbs and salt to a separate shallow dish, then mix well.
2. Place the Oour into a third shallow dish. Coat the shrimp in the flour, then the beaten egg, and finally the bread crumbs.
3. Place on a plate and repeat with all of the shrimp. Heat a skillet over high heat. Pour in enough olive oil to coat the bottom of the skillet.
4. Cook the shrimp in the hot skillet for 2 to 3 minutes on each side.
5. Remove and drain on a paper towel. Serve warm.

Per Serving:

calories: 7i 4 fats: 34.0g protein: 37.0g carbs: 63.0gJiber: 3.0g

Tomato Tuna Melts

Ingredients: *(Cook time: 4 minutes)*

- 1 (5-ounce) can chunk light tuna packed in water, drained
- 2 tablespoons plain Greek yogurt
- 2 tablespoons finely chopped celery
- 1 tablespoon finely chopped red onion
- 2 teaspoons freshly squeezed lemon juice
- Pinch cayenne pepper
- 1 large tomato, cut into '/4- inch-thick rounds
- '/2 cup shredded Cheddar cheese

Methods• *(Servings: 2*

1. Preheat the broiler to High. Stir together the tuna, yogurt, celery, red onion, lemon juice, and cayenne pepper in a medium bowl.
2. Place the tomato rounds on a baking sheet.
3. Top each with some tuna salad and Cheddar cheese.
4. Broil for 3 to 4 minutes until the cheese is melted and bubbly. Cool for 5 minutes before serving.

Per Serving

calories: 244; fat: 10.0g; protein: 30.1g; carbs: 6.9g; fiber: 1.0g

Grilled Lemon Pesto Salmon

Ingredients: *(Cook time: 6-10 minutes)*

- 10 ounces' salmon fillet (1 large piece or 2 smaller ones)
- Salt and freshly ground black pepper, to taste
- 2 tablespoons prepared pesto sauce
- 1 large fresh lemon, sliced
- Cooking spray

Methods• *(Servings:* 2

1. Reheat the grill to medium-high heat. Spray the grill grates with cooking spray.
2. Season the salmon with salt and black pepper.
3. Spread the pesto sauce on top.
4. Make a bed of fresh lemon slices about the same size as the salmon fillet on the hot grill, and place the salmon on top of the lemon slices.
5. Put any additional lemon slices on top of the salmon. Grill the salmon for 6 to 10 minutes, or until the fish is opaque and flakes apart easily. Serve hot.

Per Serving

calories: 316 fats: 21.1g protein: 29.0g carbs: 1.0g fiber: 0g

Crispy Sardines

Ingredients: *(Cook time: 5 minutes)*

- Avocado oil, as needed
- 1½ pounds whole fresh sardines, scales removed
- 1 teaspoon salt
- 1 teaspoon freshly ground black pepper
- 2 cups flour

Methods: *(Servings: 4)*

1. Preheat a deep skillet over medium heat.
2. Pour in enough oil so there is about 1 inch of it in the pan.
3. Season the fish with the salt and pepper.
4. Dredge the fish in the flour so it is completely covered.
5. Slowly drop in 1 fish at a time, making sure not to overcrowd the pan.
6. Cook for about 3 minutes on each side or just until the fish begins to brown on all sides. Serve warm.

Per Serving:

calories: 794 fats: 47g protein: 48g carbs: 44 g fiber: 2g

Trout with Lemon

Ingredients: *(Cook time: 15 minutes)*

- 4 trout fillets
- 2 tablespoons olive oil
- ½ teaspoon salt

- 1 teaspoon black pepper
- 2 garlic cloves, sliced
- 1 lemon, sliced, plus additional wedges for serving

Methods: *(Servings: 4)*

1. Preheat the air fryer to 380°F.
2. Brush each fillet with olive oil on both sides an d season with salt and pepper. Place the fillets in an even layer in the air fryer basket.
3. Place the sliced garlic over the tops of the trout fillets, then top the garlic with lemon slices and cook for 12 to 15 minutes, or until it has reached an internal tempera-ture of 145°F.
4. Serve with fresh lemon wedges.

Per Serving:

calories: 231 fats: 12g protein: 29g carbs: 1g fiber: 0g

Fettuccine with Spinach and Shrimp

Ingredients: *(Cook time: 10 minutes)*

- 8 ounces' whole-wheat fettuccine pasta, uncooked
- 3 garlic cloves, peeled, chopped
- 2 teaspoons dried basil, crushed
- 12 ounces' medium raw shrimp, peeled, deveined
- 1/4 teaspoon crushed red pepper flakes
- 1/2 cup crumbled feta cheese
- 1 teaspoon salt
- 1 package (10 ounce) frozen spinach, thawed
- 1 cup sour cream

Methods: *(Servings: 4-6)*

1. In a large-sized mixing bowl, combine sour cream, the feta, basil, garlic, salt, and red pepper.
2. According to the package instructions, cook the fettucine.
3. After the first 8 minutes of cooking, add the spinach and the shrimp to the boiling water with pasta; boil for 2 minutes more and then drain thoroughly.
4. Add the hot pasta, spinach, and shrimp mixture into the bowl with the sour cream mix; lightly toss and serve immediately.

Per Serving:

Calories 417.9, fat 18 g, protein 25.2 g, carb 39.7 g, fiber 2.5 g.

Scallop Piccata and Sautéed Spinach

Ingredients: (Cook time: 6 minutes)

- 1 (package 10-ounce) fresh baby spinach
- 1½ pounds sea scallops
- 1 garlic clove, chopped
- ½ cup vermouth
- ¼ teaspoon black pepper (freshly ground)
- ¼ teaspoon of salt
- 2 tablespoons olive oil
- 2 tablespoons fresh lemon juice
- 3 tablespoons chopped fresh parsley
- 4 teaspoons capers
- 5 teaspoons canola oil, divided

Methods: (Servings: 4)

1. Over high heat, heat a large-sized cast-iron skillet. Pat the scallops dry with paper towels. Sprinkle with salt and pepper.

2. Pour 1 tablespoon of canola oil in the pan; swirl to coat. Add the scallops; cook for about 2 minutes per side or until done or browned. Remove from the pan and keep warm.
3. Reduce the heat to medium. In the same pan, add the garlic; cooked for about 10 seconds. Add the vermouth to deglaze the pan, scraping the pan to loosen the browned bits; cook for 2 minutes more. Remove the pan from the heat.
4. Add the parsley, the lemon juice, capers, butter, stirring until the butter melts. Pour the sauce into a bowl.
5. Heat the remaining 2 teaspoons of oil in the pan over medium-high heat. Add the spinach; sauté for about 30 seconds or until the spinach is almost wilted. Drizzle the sauce over the scallops and serve with the spinach.

Per Serving:

calories 275, job 13.1 g protein 30.9 g carb 8.3 g [ther 1.8 g.

Baked Sea Bass

Ingredients: (Cook time: 12 minutes)

- 4 sea bass fillets, boneless
- Salt and black pepper to the taste
- 2 cups potato chips, crushed
- 1 tablespoon mayonnaise

Methods• (Servings: 4)

1. Season the fish fillets with salt and pepper, brush with the mayonnaise and dredge each in the potato chips.
2. Arrange the fillets on a baking sheet lined with parchment paper and bake at 400 degrees F for 12 minutes.
3. Divide the fish between plates and serve with a side salad.

calories 228, fat 8.6g, protein 25g, carbs 9.3g, fiber 0.6g

Halibut and Quinoa Mix

Ingredients: *(Cook time: 12 minutes)*

- 4 halibut fillets, boneless
- 2 tablespoons olive oil
- 1 teaspoon rosemary, dried
- 2 teaspoons cumin, ground
- 1 tablespoons coriander, ground
- 2 teaspoons cinnamon powder
- 2 teaspoons oregano, dried
- A pinch of salt and black pepper
- 2 cups quinoa, cooked
- 1 cup cherry tomatoes, halved
- 1 avocado, peeled, pitted and sliced
- 1 cucumber, cubed
- ½ cup black olives, pitted and sliced
- Juice of 1 lemon

Methods: *(Servings: 4)*

1. In a bowl, combine the fish with the rosemary, cumin, coriander, cinnamon, oregano, salt and pepper and toss.
2. Heat up a pan with the oil over medium heat, add the fish, and sear for 2 minutes on each side.
3. Introduce the pan in the oven and bake the fish at 425 degrees F for 7 minutes.
4. Meanwhile, in a bowl, mix the quinoa with the remaining ingredients, toss and divide between plates.

5. Add the fish next to the quinoa mix and serve right away.

Per Serving:

calories 364, fat 15.4g, protein 24.5g, carbs 56.4g, fiber 11.2g

Shrimp and Beans Salad

Ingredients: *(Cook time: 4 minutes)*

- 1-pound shrimp, peeled and deveined
- 30 ounces canned cannellini beans, drained and rinsed
- 2 tablespoons olive oil
- 1 cup cherry tomatoes, halved
- 1 teaspoon lemon zest, grated
- ½ cup red onion, chopped
- 4 handfuls baby arugula
- A pinch of salt and black pepper
- For the dressing: 3 tablespoons red wine vinegar
- 2 garlic cloves, minced
- ½ cup olive oil

Methods: *(Servings: 4)*

1. Heat up a pan with 2 tablespoons oil over medium-high heat, add the shrimp and cook for 2 minutes on each side.
2. In a salad bowl, combine the shrimp with the beans and the rest of the ingredients except the ones for the dressing and toss.
3. In a separate bowl, combine the vinegar with ½ cup oil and the garlic and whisk well.
4. Pour over the salad, toss and serve right away.

Per Serving:

calories 207, fat 12.3g, protein 8.7g, carbs 15.4g, fiber 6.6g

Poultry

Chicken and Olives

Ingredients: *(Cook time: 15 minutes)*

- 4 chicken breasts, skinless and boneless
- 2 tablespoons garlic, minced
- 1 tablespoon oregano, dried
- Salt and black pepper to the taste
- 2 tablespoons olive oil
- ½ cup chicken stock
- Juice of 1 lemon
- 1 cup red onion, chopped
- 1 and ½ cups tomatoes, cubed
- ¼ cup green olives, pitted and sliced
- A handful parsley, chopped

Methods: *(Servings: 4)*

1. Heat up a pan with the oil over medium-high heat, add the chicken, garlic, salt and pepper and brown for 2 minutes on each side.
2. Add the rest of the ingredients, toss, bring the mix to a simmer and cook over medium heat for 13 minutes.
3. Divide the mix between plates and serve.

Per Serving:

calories 135, fat 5.8g, protein 9.6g, carbs 12.1g, fiber 3.4g

Chicken Wrap

Ingredients: *(Cook time: 0 minutes)*

- 2 whole wheat tortilla flatbreads
- 6 chicken breast slices, skinless, boneless, cooked and shredded
- A handful baby spinach
- 2 provolone cheese slices
- 4 tomato slices
- 10 kalamata olives, pitted and sliced
- 1 red onion, sliced
- 2 tablespoons roasted peppers, chopped

Methods: *(Servings: 2)*

1. Arrange the tortillas on a working surface, and divide the chicken and the other ingredients on each.
2. Roll the tortillas and serve them right away.

Per Servings:

calories 190, fat 6.8g, protein 6.6g, carbs 15.1g, fiber 3.5g

Chicken Salad and Mustard Dressing

Ingredients: *(Cook time: 0 minutes)*

- 1 cup rotisserie chicken, skinless, boneless and cubed
- ½ cup sun-dried tomatoes, chopped
- ½ cup marinated artichoke hearts, drained and chopped
- 1 cucumber, chopped
- 1/3 cup kalamata olives, pitted and sliced
- 2 cups baby arugula

- ¼ cup parsley, chopped
- 1 avocado, peeled, pitted and cubed
- ½ cup feta cheese, crumbled
- 4 tablespoons red wine vinegar
- 2 tablespoons Dijon mustard
- 1 teaspoon basil, dried
- 1 garlic clove, minced
- 2 teaspoons honey
- ½ cup olive oil
- Salt and black pepper to the taste
- 3 tablespoons lemon juice

Methods: (*Servings: 8*)

1. In a salad bowl, mix the chicken with the tomatoes, artichokes, cucumber, olives, arugula, parsley and the avocado and toss.
2. In a different bowl, mix the vinegar with the mustard and the remaining ingredients except the cheese, whisk well, add to the salad, and toss.
3. Sprinkle the cheese on top and serve.

Per Serving:

calories 326, fat 21.7g, protein 8.8g, carbs 24.9g, fiber 1.7g

Paprika Chicken and Pineapple Mix

Ingredients: (*Cook time: 15 minutes*)

- 2 cups pineapple, peeled and cubed
- 2 tablespoons olive oil
- 1 tablespoon smoked paprika
- 2 pounds' chicken breasts, skinless, boneless and cubed
- A pinch of salt and black pepper

- 1 tablespoon chives, chopped

Methods: *(Servings: 4)*

1. Heat up a pan with the oil over medium-high heat, add the chicken, salt and pepper and brown for 4 minutes on each side.
2. Add the rest of the ingredients, toss, cook for 7 minutes more, divide everything between plates and serve with a side salad.

Per Serving:

calories 264, fat 13.2g, protein 15.4g, carbs 25.1g, fiber 8.3g

Garlic Chicken and Endives

Ingredients: *(Cook time: 15 minutes)*

- 1-pound chicken breasts, skinless, boneless and cubed
- 2 endives, sliced
- 2 tablespoons olive oil
- 4 garlic cloves, minced
- ½ cup chicken stock
- 2 tablespoons parmesan, grated
- 1 tablespoon parsley, chopped
- Salt and black pepper to the taste

Methods: *(Servings: 4)*

1. Heat up a pan with the oil over medium-high heat, add the chicken and cook for 5 minutes.
2. Add the endives, garlic, the stock, salt and pepper, stir, bring to a simmer and cook over medium-high heat for 10 minutes.
3. Add the parmesan and the parsley, toss gently, divide everything between plates and serve.

calories 280, fat 9.2g, protein 33.8g, carbs 21.6g, fiber 10.8g

Turkey Bacon Bites

Ingredients: (*Cook time: 5 minutes*)

- 4 ounces' turkey bacon, chopped
- 4 ounces Neufchatel cheese
- 1 tablespoon butter, cold jalapeno pepper, deveined and minced
- 1 teaspoon Mexican oregano tablespoons scallions, finely chopped

Methods: (*Servings: 4*)

1. Thoroughly combine all List: in a mixing bowl.
2. Roll the mixture into 8 balls.
3. To store: Divide the turkey bacon bites between two airtight containers or Ziploc bags; keep in your refrigerator for up 3 to days.

Per Serving:

calories; 16.7g fat; 2.2g carbs; 8.8g protein; 0.3g fiber 19g

Mediterranean Chicken Cucumber Salad

Ingredients: (*Cook time: 15 minutes*)

- 2 cups of packed fresh flat leaf parsley leaves
- 1 cup of fresh baby spinach
- 2 tablespoons of fresh lemon juice
- 1 tablespoon of toasted pine nuts

- 1 tablespoon of grated Parmesan cheese
- 1 medium garlic clove, smashed
- 1 teaspoon of kosher salt
- ¼ teaspoon of black pepper
- ½ cup of extra-virgin olive oil
- 4 cups of shredded rotisserie chicken
- 2 cups of cooked, shelled edamame
- 15 oz./420 g can of unsalted chickpeas, drained and rinsed
- 1 cup of chopped English cucumber
- 4 cups of arugula

Methods: *(Servings: 6)*

1. Start by putting the pine nuts, lemon juice, spinach, parsley, cheese, garlic, salt and pepper in a blender for about a minute.
2. Add a bit of olive oil and blend for another minute.
3. Take a large bowl and combine chickpeas, edamame, cucumber, and chicken together. Toss around and add an amount of pesto sauce.
4. Separate into six bowls, and top each off with a 2/3 cup of arugula an d a cup of the dressing

Per Serving:

calories: 4 82 f at: 26 g protein: 40 g carbs: 26 g fiber: 7 g

Gyro-Inspired Turkey Burgers

Ingredients: *(Cook time: 10 minutes)*

- 1 lb./453 g 93% of lean ground turkey
- ¼ cup of canola mayonnaise
- 2 teaspoons of dried oregano
- 1 teaspoon of ground cumin

- '/4 teaspoon of kosher salt
- '/4 teaspoon black pepper, divided into two
- '/ teaspoons
- Cooking spray
- '/s cup plain of whole-milk
- Greek yogurt
- '/3 cup of chopped kalamata olives
- 1 tablespoon of fresh lemon juice
- 4 whole-wheat hamburger buns
- 2 cups of arugula
- '/2 cup of sliced cucumber
- '/2 cup of thinly sliced red onion

Methods• (Servings: 4)

1. Combine turkey, cumin, mayo, oregano, teaspoon pepper, and salt and make 4 medium patties.
2. Place a non-stick skillet on a medium-high temperature and coat with a tablespoon of olive oil.
3. Cook each burger for around 5 minutes per side, until they are golden brown.
4. Combine yogurt, olives, lemon juice, salt and the last teaspoon of pepper in a bowl to make a dressing. Spread it over both the top and bottom of the bun.
5. Follow up by placing arugula, the cooked burger, red onion, and cucumber.

Per Serving

calories: 37$ fats: 17 g protein: 22 g carbs: 28 g f ther: 4 g

Grilled Chicken and Rustic Mustard Cream

Ingredients: *(Cook time: 12 minutes)*

- 1 tablespoon plus 1 teaspoon whole-grain Dijon mustard, divided

- 1 tablespoon water
- 1 teaspoon fresh rosemary, chopped
- ¼ teaspoon black pepper
- ¼ teaspoon of salt
- 1 tablespoon olive oil
- 3 tablespoons light mayonnaise
- 4 pieces (6-ounces each) chicken breast halves, skinless, boneless
- Rosemary sprigs (optional)
- Cooking spray

Methods: (Servings: 4)

1. Preheat the grill.
2. In a small-sized bowl, combine the olive oil, 1-teaspoon of mustard; brush evenly over each chicken breast.
3. Coat the grill rack with the cooking spray, place and chicken, and grill for 6 minutes per side or until cooked.
4. While the chicken is grilling, combine the mayonnaise, the 1 tablespoon of mustard, and the water in a bowl.
5. Serve the grilled chicken with the mustard cream. If desired garnish with some rosemary sprigs.

Per Serving:

calories 26, fat 10 g protein 39.6 g, carb 1.7 g., fiber 0.2 g.

Greek-Style Turkey Burgers

Ingredients: (Cook time: 10 minutes)

- 4 whole-wheat French hamburger buns, split, toasted
- Olive oil cooking spray
- Toppings: *Lettuce leaves, thinly sliced, Cucumber, tomato slices,*

- Garnish: *Pepperoncini salad peppers*

For the burger:

- 1 1/3 pounds ground turkey breast
- 1 package (4 ounces) feta cheese, crumbled
- 1/4 cup red onion, finely chopped
- 1 teaspoon dried oregano
- 1 teaspoon lemon zest
- 1/2 teaspoon salt

For the cucumber sauce:

- 1/2 teaspoon salt
- 1/2 cup English cucumber, grated
- 1 tablespoon fresh mint, chopped
- 1 container (6 ounces) Greek yogurt, fat-free

Methods• (Servings: 4)

1. In a bowl, mix the burger ingredients until well combined; shape into 4 pieces 1/2-inch thick burger patties.
2. Over medium-high heat, heat a grill pan.
3. Coat the grill pan with the olive oil cooking spray. Place the patties; cook for about 5 minutes per side or until cooked.
4. Serve the burger patties between buns, topped with cucumber sauce, and with your preferred toppings. If desired, garnish.

Per Serving:

calories 386, fat 13.7 g protein 30.2 g carb 34 g fiber 2.3 g.

Lemon-Simmered Chicken & Artichokes

Ingredients: *(Cook time: 10-15 minutes)*

- 4 boneless chicken breast halves, skins removed
- 1/4 tsp. Himalayan salt
- 1/4 tsp. freshly ground black pepper
- 2 tsp. avocado oil
- 1 tbsp. lemon juice
- 2 tsp. dried crushed oregano
- 1/4 cup olives, pitted and halved
- 2/3 cup reduced-sodium chicken stock
- 14 oz. canned, water-packed, quartered artichoke hearts

Methods: *(Servings: 4)*

1. Sprinkle the chicken with salt and pepper. Brown the chicken in a pan for 2 to 4 minutes.
2. When the chicken is nicely browned, stir in the chicken stock, oregano, olives, lemon juice, and artichoke hearts.
3. Bring it to a boil. Then lower the heat.
4. Simmer with a lid on the pan for 4-5 minutes. Serve hot.

Per Serving:

calories: 225 fats: 9g protein: 2 carb: 9g

Spicy, Yogurt-Marinated Chicken Skewers

Ingredients: *(Cook time: 12 minutes)*

- 1½ tbsp. Aleppo pepper (extra for garnish)
- 3 tsp. crushed garlic

- 1 tsp. freshly ground black pepper
- 2 tsp. Himalayan salt
- 2 tbsp. tomato paste
- 2 tbsp. balsamic vinegar
- 3 tbsp. extra-virgin olive oil (extra for brushing)
- 1 cup plain Greek yogurt
- 1$3/4$lb. boneless chicken breasts, skins removed, cubed
- 2 unpeeled lemons, thinly sliced (divided)

Methods• (Servings: 4-6)

1. Place the Aleppo pepper in a bowl, along with 1 tablespoon of warm water, and let stand for 5 minutes.
2. Whisk in the garlic, pepper, salt, tomato paste, vinegar, olive oil, and yogurt. Add the chicken and half of the lemon slices. To coat, toss everything together. Cover the bowl in cling wrap, and chill overnight.
3. To prevent charring, soak 10—12 wooden skewers in a bowl of water for 20 minutes. Brush a grill with extra olive oil, and heat it on medium-high.
4. When the grill is nice and hot, thread the chicken onto the soaked skewers, discarding the excess marinade.
5. Grill the skewers for 10—12 minutes, turning at regular intervals, until the chicken is cooked all the way through and nicely browned on all sides. Serve the skewers hot on a bed of lemon slices.

Per Serving:

calories: 301 fats: 11g carbs: kg protein: 25g

Ground Turkey Mince

Ingredients: (Cook time: 10-IS minutes)

- 2 tbsp. avocado oil

- 1 lb. lean ground turkey
- 2 tsp. crushed garlic
- 1 bell pepper, seeded and diced
- 1 small shallot, chopped
- '/2 tsp. ground cumin
- '/2 tsp. ground cinnamon
- Freshly ground black pepper
- '/4 tsp. kosher salt
- 2 tbsp. hummus
- '/4 cup chicken bone broth
- 1 lemon, finely zested
- 1 tbsp. lemon juice
- Fresh parsley, chopped, for garnish

Methods• *(Servings: 4)*

1. Heat 1 tbsp. of the oil in a pan. Add the ground turkey, and fry for about 5 minutes in a single layer, without stirring.
2. After 5 minutes, flip the meat over and stir to separate all the bits. Scrape into a bowl, and set aside. Return the pan to a low heat.
3. Then add the remaining oil. Fry the garlic, bell peppers, and shallots for about 5 minutes.
4. Stir in the cumin and cinnamon for about 30 seconds before adding the ground turkey back to the pan, along with a pinch of pepper, salt, hummus, chicken broth, lemon zest, and lemon juice. Stir for 5 minutes.
5. Serve the ground turkey on the wraps of your choice, garnished with fresh parsley.

Per Serving:

calories: 280 fats: 1 kg protein: 23g carbs: 10g

Classic Fajita Chicken Strips

Ingredients: (*Cook time: 15 minutes*)

- Cooking spray
- 1 tbsp. olive oil
- 1 pound boneless, skinless chicken tenderloins, cut into strips
- 3 bell peppers, any color, cut into chunks
- 1 onion, cut into chunks
- 1 tbsp. fajita seasoning mix

Methods: (*Servings: 4*)

1. Preheat the air fryer to 370ºF.
2. In a large bowl, mix together the chicken, bell peppers, onion, olive oil, and fajita seasoning mix until completely coated.
3. Spray the air fryer basket lightly with cooking spray.
4. Place the chicken and vegetables in the air fryer basket and lightly spray with cooking spray.
5. Air fry for 7 minutes. Shake the basket and air fry for an additional 5 to 8 minutes, until the chicken is cooked through and the veggies are starting to char. Serve warm.

Per Serving:

calories: 182, fat: 6 g, protein: 25 g, carbs: 8 g, fiber: 2 g

Roasted Red Pepper Chicken with Lemony Garlic Hummus

Ingredients: (*Cook time: 10 minutes*)

- 1¼ pounds boneless, skinless chicken thighs, cut into 1-inch pieces

- '/2 sweet or red onion, cut into 1-inch chunks
- 2 tablespoons extra-virgin olive oil
- '/2 teaspoon dried thyme
- '/4 teaspoon freshly ground black pepper
- '/4 teaspoon kosher or sea salt
- 1 (12-ounce) jar roasted red peppers, drained and chopped
- Lemony Garlic Hummus, or a 10-ounce container prepared hummus
- '/2 medium lemon
- 3 (6-inch) whole-wheat pita breads, cut into eighths

Methods• *(Servings: 6)*

1. Line a large, rimmed baking sheet with aluminum foil. Set aside. Set one oven rack about 4 inches below the broiler element. Preheat the broiler to high.
2. In a large bowl, mix together the chicken, onion, oil, thyme, pepper, and salt. Spread the mixture onto the prepared baking sheet.
3. Place the chicken under the broiler and broil for 5 minutes. Remove the pan, stir in the red peppers, and return to the broiler. Broil for another 5 minutes, or until the chicken and onion just start to char on the tips. Remove from the oven.
4. Spread the hummus onto a large serving platter, and spoon the chicken mixture on top. Squeeze the juice from half a lemon over the top, and serve with the pita pieces.

Per Serving:

calories: 324; fat: 11g; protein: 29g; carbs: 29g; fiber: 6g

Tahini Chicken Rice Bowls

Ingredients: *(Cook time: 1$ minutes)*

- 1 cup uncooked instant brown rice
- '/4 cup tahini or peanut butter

- '/4 cup 2% plain Greek yogurt
- 2 tablespoons chopped scallions, green and white parts
- 1 tablespoon freshly squeezed lemon juice
- 1 tablespoon water
- 1 teaspoon ground cumin
- '/4 teaspoon ground cinnamon
- '/4 teaspoon kosher or sea salt
- 2 cups chopped cooked chicken breast
- '/2 cup chopped dried apricots
- 2 cups peeled and chopped seedless cucumber
- 4 teaspoons sesame seeds
- Fresh mint leaves, for serving (optional)

Methods• (Servings: 4)

1. Cook the brown rice according to the package instructions.
2. While the rice is cooking, in a medium bowl, mix together the tahini, yogurt, scallions, lemon juice, water, cumin, cinnamon, and salt.
3. Transfer half the tahini mixture to another medium bowl. Mix the chicken into the first bowl.
4. When the rice is done, mix it into the second bowl of tahini (the one without the chicken).
5. To assemble, divide the chicken among four bowls. Spoon the rice mixture next to the chicken in each bowl.
6. Next to the chicken, place the dried apricots, and in the remaining empty section, add the cucumbers. Sprinkle with sesame seeds, and top with mint, if desired, and serve.

Per Serving:

calories: 420; fat: 13g; protein: 29g; carbs: 46g; fiber: 8g

Grape Chicken Panzanella

Ingredients: (Cook time: $ minutes)

- 3 cups day-old bread cut into 1-inch cubes
- 5 tablespoons extra-virgin olive oil, divided
- 2 cups chopped cooked chicken breast
- 1 cup red seedless grapes, halved
- 1/2 pint grape or cherry tomatoes, halved
- 1/2 cup Gorgonzola cheese crumbles
- 1/8 cup chopped walnuts
- 1/4 cup diced red onion
- 3 tablespoons chopped fresh mint leaves
- 1/4 teaspoon freshly ground black pepper
- 1 tablespoon balsamic vinegar
- Zest and juice of
- 1 small lemon
- 1 teaspoon honey

Methods• (Servings: 6)

1. Line a large, rimmed baking sheet with aluminum foil. Set aside. Set one oven rack about 4 inches below the broiler element. Preheat the broiler to high.
2. In a large serving bowl, drizzle the cubed bread with 2 tablespoons of oil, and mix gently with your hands to coat. Spread the mixture over the prepared baking sheet.
3. Place the baking sheet under the broiler for 2 minutes. Stir the bread, then broil for another 30 to 60 seconds, watching carefully so the bread pieces are toasted and not burned. Remove from the oven and set aside.
4. In the same (now empty) large serving bowl, mix together the chicken, grapes, tomatoes, Gorgonzola, walnuts, onion, mint, and pepper. Add the toasted bread pieces, and gently mix together.

5. In a small bowl, whisk together the remaining 3 tablespoons of oil, vinegar, zest and juice from the lemon, and honey.
6. Drizzle the dressing over the salad, toss gently to mix, and serve.

Per Serving:

calories:380; fat: 2Jg; carb: 23g

Turkey Burgers with Mango Salsa

Ingredients: (Cook time: 10 minutes)

- 1'/2 pounds ground turkey breast
- 1 teaspoon sea salt, divided
- '/4 teaspoon freshly ground black pepper
- 2 tablespoons extra-virgin olive oil
- 2 mangos, peeled, pitted, and cubed
- '/2 red onion, finely chopped
- Juice of 1 lime
- 1 garlic clove, minced
- '/2 jalapeño pepper, seeded and finely minced
- 2 tablespoons chopped fresh cilantro leaves

Methods• (Servings: 6)

1. Form the turkey breast into 4 patties and season with '/2teaspoon of sea salt and the pepper.
2. In a large nonstick skillet over medium-high heat, heat the olive oil until it shimmers.
3. Add the turkey patties and cook for about 5 minutes per side until browned.
4. While the patties cook, mix together the mango, red onion, lime juice, garlic, jalapeño, cilantro, and remaining '/2teaspoon of sea salt in a small bowl.
5. Spoon the salsa over the turkey patties and serve.

Per Serving:

calories: 384; fat: 16g; protein: 34g; carbs: 27g; fiber: 3g

Meat

Pork Chops and Relish

Ingredients: (*Cook time: 14 minutes*)

- 6 pork chops, boneless
- 7 ounces marinated artichoke hearts, chopped and their liquid reserved
- A pinch of salt and black pepper
- 1 teaspoon hot pepper sauce
- 1 and ½ cups tomatoes, cubed
- 1 jalapeno pepper, chopped
- ½ cup roasted bell peppers, chopped
- ½ cup black olives, pitted and sliced

Methods: (*Servings: 6*)

1. In a bowl, mix the chops with the pepper sauce, reserved liquid from the artichokes, cover and keep in the fridge for 15 minutes.
2. Heat up a grill over medium-high heat, add the pork chops and cook for 7 minutes on each side.
3. In a bowl, combine the artichokes with the peppers and the remaining ingredients, toss, divide on top of the chops and serve.

Per Serving:

calories 215, fat 6, protein 35, carbs 6, fiber 1

Crispy Beef Schnitzel

Ingredients: (*Cook time: 12 minutes*)

- 2 tbsps. olive oil

- 1 thin beef schnitzel
- 1 egg, beaten
- ½ cup friendly bread crumbs
- Pepper and salt, to taste

Methods: (Servings: 1)

1. Preheat the air fryer to 350°F.
2. In a shallow dish, combine the bread crumbs, oil, pepper, and salt. In a second shallow dish, place the beaten egg.
3. Dredge the schnitzel in the egg before rolling it in the bread crumbs.
4. Put the coated schnitzel in the air fryer basket and air fry for 12 minutes.
5. Flip the schnitzel halfway through. Serve immediately.

Per Serving:

calories: 618, fat: 44 g, protein: 39 g, carbs: 22 g, fiber: 1 g

Pork Chops and Cherries Mix

Ingredients: (Cook time: 12 minutes)

- 4 pork chops, boneless
- Salt and black pepper to the taste
- ½ cup cranberry juice
- 1 and ½ teaspoons spicy mustard
- ½ cup dark cherries, pitted and halved
- Cooking spray

Methods: (Servings: 4)

1. Heat up a pan greased with the cooking spray over medium-high heat.
2. Add the pork chops, cook them for 5 minutes on each side and divide between plates.

3. Heat up the same pan over medium heat.
4. Add the cranberry juice and the rest of the ingredients, whisk, bring to a simmer.
5. Cook for 2 minutes, drizzle over the pork chops and serve.

Per Serving:

calories 262, fat 8g, protein 30g, carbs 16g, fiber 1g

Simple Strip Steak

Ingredients: (Cook time: 10 minutes)

- 1 tsp. olive oil
- 1 (9½-ounces) strip steak
- Crushed red pepper flakes, to taste
- Salt and black pepper, to taste

Methods: (Servings: 2)

1. Preheat the Air fryer to 400ºF and grease an Air fryer basket.
2. Rub the steak generously with red pepper flakes, salt and black pepper and coat with olive oil.
3. Transfer the steak in the Air fryer basket and roast for about 10 minutes, flipping once in between.
4. Dish out the steak and cut into desired size slices to serve.

Per Serving:

calories: 382, fat: 24 g, protein: 38 g, carbs: 0 g, fiber: 0 g

Pork Chops and Herbed Tomato Sauce

Ingredients: (Cook time: 10 minutes)

- 4 pork loin chops, boneless
- 6 tomatoes, peeled and crushed
- 3 tablespoons parsley, chopped
- 2 tablespoons olive oil
- ¼ cup kalamata olives, pitted and halved
- 1 yellow onion, chopped
- 1 garlic clove, minced

Methods: (*Servings: 4*)

1. Heat up a pan with the oil over medium heat.
2. Add the pork chops, cook them for 3 minutes on each side and divide between plates.
3. Heat up the same pan again over medium heat.
4. Add the tomatoes, parsley and the rest of the ingredients, whisk, simmer for 4 minutes.
5. Drizzle over the chops and serve.

Per Serving:

calories 334, fat 17g, protein 34g, carbs 12g, fiber 2g

Beef Tips with Onion

Ingredients: (*Cook time: 10 minutes*)

- 1 tbsp. avocado oil
- 1-pound top round beef, cut into 1½-inch cubes
- ½ yellow onion, chopped
- 2 tbsps. Worcestershire sauce
- 1 tsp. garlic powder
- 1 tsp. onion powder
- Salt and black pepper, to taste

1. Preheat the Air fryer to 360°F and grease an Air fryer basket.
2. Mix the beef tips, onion, Worcestershire sauce, avocado oil, and spices in a bowl.
3. Arrange the beef mixture in the Air fryer basket and roast for about 10 minutes.
4. Dish out the steak mixture onto serving plates and cut into desired size slices to serve.

Per Serving:

calories: 4$3, fat: 25 g protein: 48 g carbs: $ g fiber: 1 g

Pork, Greens and Corn

Ingredients: (Cook time: 0 minutes)

- 1 red chili, chopped
- 2 tablespoons balsamic vinegar
- 1 tablespoon lime juice
- 1 teaspoon olive oil
- 4 ounces mixed salad greens
- 2 ounces' corn
- 1 green bell pepper, cut into strips
- 4 ounces' pork stew meat, cooked and cut in thin strips

Methods• (Servings: 4)

1. In a bowl, combine the pork with the bell pepper and the rest of the ingredients, toss and keep in the fridge for 10 minutes before serving.
2. Divide the mix between plates and serve.

Per Servings•

calories 283, fat 14.6g protein 13.9g carbs 23.1g fiber 10.6g

Balsamic Ground Lamb

Ingredients: (Cook time: 12 minutes)

- Salt and black pepper to the taste
- 2 tablespoons olive oil
- 6 scallions, chopped
- 2 tablespoons ginger, grated
- 2 garlic cloves, minced
- 1-pound lamb stew, ground
- 1 tablespoon chili paste
- 2 tablespoons balsamic vinegar
- ¼ cup chicken stock
- ¼ cup dill, chopped

Methods: (Servings: 4)

1. Heat up a pan with the oil over medium high-heat, add the scallions, stir and sauté for 3 minutes.
2. Add the meat and brown for 3 minutes more.
3. Add the rest of the ingredients, toss, cook for 6 minutes more.
4. Divide into bowls and serve.

Per Serving:

calories 303, fat 13.4g, protein 19.2g, carbs 15.2g, fiber 9.4g

Pork Salad

Ingredients: (Cook time: 10 minutes)

- 1-pound pork loin, cut into strips
- 3 scallions, chopped
- 1 cucumber, sliced
- 1 red chili, sliced
- 1 tablespoon coriander leaves, chopped
- 2 ounces' walnuts, chopped
- 2 tablespoons olive oil
- Salt and black pepper to the taste
- Juice of 1 lime
- 1 garlic clove, minced

Methods: *(Servings: 4)*

1. Heat up a pan with half of the oil over medium-high heat.
2. Add the meat, cook for 5 minutes on each side and transfer to a bowl.
3. Add the rest of the ingredients to the bowl as well, and toss together.
4. Serve and enjoy.

Per Serving:

calories 267, fat 13.3g, protein 17.6g, carbs 15.2g, fiber 8.2g

Minty Balsamic Lamb

Ingredients: *(Cook time: 11 minutes)*

- 2 red chilies, chopped
- 2 tablespoons balsamic vinegar
- 1 cup mint leaves, chopped
- Salt and black pepper to the taste
- 2 tablespoons olive oil
- 4 lamb fillets
- 1 tablespoon sweet paprika

1. Heat up a pan with half of the oil over medium-high heat.
2. Add the chilies, the vinegar and the rest of the ingredients except the lamb, whisk and cook over medium heat for 5 minutes.
3. Brush the lamb with the rest of the oil, season with salt and black pepper, place on preheated grill and cook over medium heat for 3 minutes on each side.
4. Divide the lamb between plates, drizzle the minty vinaigrette all over and serve.

Per Serving:

calories 312, Fat *12.1g, protein 17.2g, carbs 17.kg, fiber 9.1g*

Pork Kebabs

Ingredients: (Cook time: 14 minutes)

-   1 yellow onion, chopped
-   1-pound pork meat, ground
-   3 tablespoons cilantro, chopped
-   1 tablespoon lime juice
-   1 garlic clove, minced
-   2 teaspoon oregano, dried
-   Salt and black pepper to the taste
-   A drizzle of olive oil

Methods• (Servings: 6)

1. In a bowl, mix the pork with the other ingredients except the oil, stir well and shape medium kebabs out of this mix.
2. Divide the kebabs on skewers, and brush them with a drizzle of oil.
3. Place the kebabs on your preheated grill and cook over medium heat for 7 minutes on each side.

4. Divide the kebabs between plates and serve with a side salad.

calories 229, fat 14g, protein 12.4g, carbs 13.3g, fiber 8.3g

Beef Shawarma

Ingredients: *(Cook time: $ minutes)*

- '/2 lb. ground beef
- '/4 tsp cinnamon
- '/2 tsp dried oregano
- 1 cup cabbage, cut into strips
- '/2 cup bell pepper, sliced
- '/4 tsp ground coriander
- '/2 tsp cumin
- '/4 tsp cayenne pepper
- '/4 tsp ground allspice
- '/2 cup onion, chopped
- '/2 tsp Salt

Methods• *(Servings: 2*

1. Set the instant pot to sauté mode.
2. Add the meat to the pot and sauté until brown.
3. Add the remaining ingredients and stir well.
4. Cook for 5 minutes on high, covered.
5. Stir and serve.

Per Serving:

calories: 243 fats: 7.4g protein: 3$.6g carbs: 7.9g

Greek-Style Lamb Burgers

Ingredients: (Cook time: 10 minutes)

- 1-pound ground lamb
- ½ teaspoon salt
- ½ teaspoon freshly ground black pepper
- 4 tablespoons crumbled feta cheese
- Buns, toppings, and tzatziki, for serving (optional)

Methods: (Servings: 4)

1. Preheat the grill to high heat. In a large bowl, using your hands, combine the lamb with the salt and pepper. Divide the meat into 4 portions.
2. Divide e ach portion in half to make a top and a bottom. Flatten each half into a 3-inch circle. Make a dent in the center of one of the halves and place 1 tablespoon of the feta cheese in the center.
3. Place the second half of the patty on top of the feta cheese and press down to close the 2 halves together, making it resemble a round burger.
4. Grill each side for 3 minutes, for medium-well. Serve on a bun with your favorite toppings and tzatziki sauce, if desired.

Per Serving:

calories: 345 fats: 29.0g protein: 20.0g carbs: 1.0g fiber: 0g

Beef, Tomato, and Lentils Stew

Ingredients: (Cook time: 10 minutes)

- 1 tablespoon extra-virgin olive oil

- 1-pound extra-lean ground beef
- 1 onion, chopped
- 1 (14-ounce) can chopped tomatoes with garlic and basil, drained
- 1 (14-ounce) can lentils, drained
- 1/2 teaspoon sea salt
- 1/ teaspoon freshly ground black pepper

Methods• *(Servings: 4)*

1. Heat the olive oil in a pot over medium-high heat until shimmering.
2. Add the beef and onion to the pot and sauté for 5 minutes or until the beef is lightly browned.
3. Add the remaining ingredients. Bring to a boil. Reduce the heat to medium and cook for 4 more minutes or until the lentils are tender. I(eep stirring during the cooking.
4. Pour them in a large serving bowl and serve immediately.

Per Serving:

calories: 460 fats: 14.8g protein: 44.2g carbs: 36.9gJibcr: 17.0g

Beef Spanakopita Pita Pockets

Ingredients: *(Cook time: 1$ minutes)*

- 3 teaspoons extra-virgin olive oil, divided
- 1-pound ground beef(93% lean)
- 2 garlic cloves, minced (about 1 teaspoon)
- 2 (6-ounce) bags baby spinach, chopped (about 12 cups)
- 1/2 cup crumbled feta cheese (about 2 ounces)
- 1/s cup ricotta cheese
- 1/2 teaspoon ground nutmeg
- 1/4 teaspoon freshly ground black pepper

- '/4 cup slivered almonds
- 4 (6-inch) whole-wheat pita breads, cut in half

Methods• *(Servings: 4)*

1. In a large skillet over medium heat, heat 1 teaspoon of oil. Add the ground beef and cook for 10 minutes, breaking it up with a wooden spoon and stirring occasionally. Remove from the heat and drain in a colander. Set the meat aside.
2. Place the skillet back on the heat, and add the remaining 2 teaspoons of oil. Add the garlic and cook for 1 minute, stirring constantly. Add the spinach and cook for 2 to 3 minutes, or until the spinach has cooked down, stirring often.
3. Turn off the heat and mix in the feta cheese, ricotta, nutmeg, and pepper. Stir until all the ingredients are well incorporated. Mix in the almonds.
4. Divide the beef filling among the eight pita pocket halves to stuff them and serve.

Per Serving:

calories: $06; fat: 22g; protein: 39g; carbs: 42g

Kofta Kebabs

Ingredients: *(Cook time: 12 minutes)*

- '/2 lb. ground beef/lamb
- 1 garlic clove, minced
- 1 small red onion, finely chopped
- '/4 tsp. nutmeg
- '/4 tsp. allspice
- '/4 tsp. paprika
- '/ tsp. ground black pepper
- '/4 tsp. cumin
- '/4 tsp. cardamom

- '/4 tsp. sea salt

Methods• *(Servings:* 2

1. Mix all the ingredients in a food processor. Shape 4 oval koftas using your hand. If you prefer, you can string the meat on skewers.
2. Arrange the koftas on a grill or in an air fryer basket in a single layer. Cook at 350°F (178°C) for 12 minutes until golden brown, flipping once.
3. Serve kofta kebabs with pita bread and grilled vegetables. They perfectly pair with tahini sauce/baba ganoush/tzatziki sauce/hummus.

Per Serving:

calories: 161, fat: 4.6 g protein: 23.1 g carbs: 4 g fiber: 1 g

Salads and Side Dish

Couscous Salad

Ingredients: (Cook time: 10 minutes)

- 1 cup red kidney beans, canned
- 1 cup couscous
- 1 cup feta cheese
- 1/3 cup green onion
- 1/4 cup pine nuts
- 2 medium tomatoes, diced
- 2 tablespoons lemon juice
- 2 tablespoons olive oil
- 2 tablespoons oregano

Methods:

1. Cook the couscous in the in the water; let cool to room temperature.
2. Whisk the olive oil and the lemon juice together.
3. Pour all of the ingredients into the couscous; season with freshly cracked pepper.

Per Serving:

Calories 448.6, fat 21.1g, carb 50g, fiber 7.1g, 5 g protein 16.1 g.

Zucchini and Cherry Tomato Salad

Ingredients: (Cook time: 5 minutes)

- 1 medium zucchini, shredded or sliced paper thin
- 6 cherry tomatoes, halved

- 3-4 basil leaves, thinly sliced
- 2 tbsps. freshly grated, low-fat Parmesan cheese
- 3 tbsps. olive oil
- Juice of 1 lemon
- Sea salt and freshly ground pepper

Methods: *(Servings: 2):*

1. Place the zucchini slices on 2 plates in even layers. Top with the tomatoes.
2. Drizzle with lemon juice and olive oil. Season to taste.
3. Top with the basil and sprinkle with cheese. Serve.

Per Serving:

Calories: 211, Fat: 21 g, Protein: 2 g, Carbs: 5 g

Chickpea Salad

Ingredients: *(Cook time: 0 minutes)*

- 1 garlic clove, minced
- 1 green pepper, julienned
- 1 pinch pepper
- 1 pinch salt
- 1 teaspoon Dijon mustard
- ½ cup stuffed green olive
- ½ red pepper, julienned
- 1/3 cup olive oil
- 2 cans (19 ounces each) chickpeas, rinsed (or white kidney beans)
- 2 tablespoons balsamic vinegar
- 2 tablespoons capers (optional)

Methods: *(Servings: 4-6):*

1. In a bowl, whisk the olive oil, mustard, vinegar, garlic, salt, and pepper.

2. Add the remaining ingredients; gently fold until the vegetables are evenly coated.
3. Serve over your preferred greens.

Per serving:

Calories 499, fat 21.2g protein 13.9 g carb 63g., fiber 12.7.

Pepper and Tomato Salad

Ingredients: (Cook time: 10 minutes)

- 2 cloves garlic, minced
- 4 large tomatoes, seeded and diced
- 3 large yellow peppers
- '/4 cup olive oil
- 1 small bunch fresh basil leaves
- Sea salt and freshly ground pepper

Methods• (Servings: 6)

Preheat broiler to high heat and broil the peppers until blackened.

Remove from heat and place peppers in a paper bag. Seal and cool down peppers.

Peel the skins off the peppers, then seed and chop them.

Add half of the peppers to a food processor with olive oil, basil, and garlic, and pulse several times to make the dressing.

Mix the rest of the peppers with the tomatoes and toss with the dressing.

Season the salad with sea salt and freshly ground pepper. Serve with room temperature.

Per Serving:

Calories: 113, Fat: 9 g, Protein: 2 g, Carbs: 7 g

Cauliflower & Tomato Salad

Ingredients: *(Cook time: 15 minutes)*

- 1 Head Cauliflower, Chopped
- 2 tbsp. Parsley, Fresh & chopped
- 2 Cups Cherry Tomatoes, Halved
- 2 tbsp. Lemon Juice, Fresh
- 2 tbsp. Pine Nuts
- Sea Salt & Black Pepper to Taste

Methods: (Servings: 4)

1. Mix your lemon juice, cherry tomatoes, cauliflower and parsley together, and then season.
2. Top with pine nuts, and mix well before serving.

Per Serving:

Calories: 64 Fat: 3.3 g Protein: 2.8 g Carbs: 7.9 g

Tuna Salad

Ingredients: *(Cook time: 0 minutes)*

12 oz. canned tuna in water, drained and flaked

¼ cup roasted red peppers, chopped

2 tbsp. capers, drained

8 kalamata olives, pitted and sliced

2 tbsp. olive oil

1 tbsp. parsley, chopped

1 tbsp.lemon juice

A pinch of salt and black pepper

Methods: (Servings: 2)

In a bowl, combine the tuna with roasted peppers and the rest of the ingredients.

Toss to combine, divide between plates and serve for breakfast.

Enjoy!

Per Serving:

Calories 2$0, Fat 17.$ g Protein 10.4 g, Carbs 2.6 g

Corn and Shrimp Salad

Ingredients: (Cook time: 10 minutes)

- 4 ears of sweet corn, husked
- 1 avocado, peeled, pitted and chopped
- 1/2 cup basil, Chopped
- A pinch of salt and black pepper
- 1 lb. shrimp, peeled and deveined
- 1 and 1/2 cups cherry tomatoes, halved
- 1/4 cup olive oil

Methods• (Servings: 4)

1. Put the corn in a pot, add water to cover, bring to a boil over medium heat, cook for 6 minutes, drain, cool down, cut corn from the cob and put it in a bowl.
2. Thread the shrimp onto skewers and brush with some of the oil.
3. Place the skewers on the preheated grill, cook over medium heat for 2 minutes on each side, remove from skewers and add over the corn.
4. Add the rest of the ingredients to the bowl, toss, divide between plates and serve for breakfast.

Per Serving:

Calories 316; fat: 22g; Protein: 1$g Carbs: 24g

Baked Acorn Squash and Arugula Salad

Ingredients: *(Cook time: 0 minutes)*

- Extra-virgin olive oil, for coating squash
- 4 cups arugula
- 1 medium acorn squash, cut into rounds
- '/2 cup Brussels sprouts, shaved or thinly sliced
- ^{1} cup pomegranate seeds
- '/4 cup pumpkin seeds

Methods• *(Servings: 3)*

1. Preheat the oven to 400°F.
2. Line a baking sheet with parchment paper. Arrange the acorn squash on the baking sheet and slowly toss with olive oil to coat well. Place in a single layer and bake for about 20 to 25 minutes, until squash is tender.
3. Meanwhile, combine the arugula, Brussels sprouts, pomegranate, and pumpkin seeds in a bowl, and toss with the dressing of choice.
4. Place acorn squash on top and drizzle additional dressing on top. Enjoy!

Per Serving:

Calories: 351, Fat: 22 g, Protein: 8 g, Carbs: 34 g

Cucumber Gazpacho

Ingredients: *(Cook time: 0 minutes)*

- 2 cucumbers, peeled, deseeded, and cut into chunks
- ½ cup mint, finely chopped
- 2 cups plain Greek yogurt
- 2 garlic cloves, minced
- 2 cups low-sodium vegetable soup
- 1 tablespoon no-salt-added tomato paste
- 3 teaspoons fresh dill
- Sea salt and freshly ground pepper, to taste

Methods: *(Servings: 4)*

1. Put the cucumber, mint, yogurt, and garlic in a food processor, then pulse until creamy and smooth.
2. Transfer the puréed mixture in a large serving bowl, then add the vegetable soup, tomato paste, dill, salt, and ground black pepper. Stir to mix well.
3. Keep the soup in the refrigerator for at least 2 hours, then serve chilled

Per Serving:

Calories: 133; Fat: 1.5g; Protein: 14.2g; Carbs: 16.5g

Cheesy Roasted Broccolini

Ingredients: *(Cook time: 10 minutes)*

- 1 bunch broccolini (about 5 ounces)
- 1 tablespoon olive oil
- '/2 teaspoon garlic powder
- '/4 teaspoon salt
- 2 tablespoons grated
- Romano cheese

Methods• *(Servings:* 2

1. Preheat the oven to 400°F. Lin e a sheet pan with parchment paper.
2. Slice the tough ends off the broccolini and put in a medium bowl. Add the olive oil, garlic powder, and salt and toss to coat well. Arrange the broccolini on the prepared sheet pan.
3. Roast in the preheated oven for 7 minutes, flipping halfway through the cooking time.
4. Remove the pan from the oven and sprinkle the cheese over the broccolini. Using tongs, carefully flip the broccolini over to coat all sides.
5. Return to the oven and cook for an additional 2 to 3 minutes, or until the cheese melts and starts to turn golden. Serve warm.

per serving:

Calories: 114; Fat: 9.0g; Protein: 4.0g; Carbs: 3.0g

Meatballs Platter

Ingredients: *(Cook time: 1$ minutes)*

- 1-pound beef meat, ground
- '/4 cup panko breadcrumbs
- A pinch of salt and black pepper
- 3 tablespoons red onion, grated
- '/4 cup parsley, chopped

154

- 2 garlic cloves, minced
- tablespoons lemon juice
- Zest of 1 lemon, grated egg
- ½ teaspoon cumin, ground
- ½ teaspoon coriander, ground
- ¼ teaspoon cinnamon powder
- 2 ounces' feta cheese, crumbled

Methods: *(Serving: 4)*

1. In a bowl, mix the beef with the breadcrumbs, salt, pepper, and the rest of the ingredients except the cooking spray, stir well and shape medium balls out of this mix.
2. Arrange the meatballs on a baking sheet lined with parchment paper, grease them with cooking spray and bake at 450° F f or 15 minutes.
3. Put the meatballs on a platter and serve as an appetizer.

Per Serving:

Calories 300; Fat 15.4 g; Protein 35 g; Carbs 22.4 g

Balsamic Mushrooms

Ingredients: *(Cook time: 7 minutes)*

- 1-pound white mushroom, halved (or quartered if they are very large)
- 1 teaspoon salt
- 1/4 cup olive oil
- 1/4 teaspoon red pepper flakes
- 3 tablespoons balsamic vinegar Pepper, to taste

Methods: *(Serving: 4-6)*

1. In a medium-sized skillet, heat the oil over medium high-heat. Add the mushrooms; cook for about 5 minutes or until golden.
2. Stir in the vinegar, red pepper Oakes, and the salt, then season with pepper; cook for 1 minute more.
3. Transfer into a serving bowl.
4. *Notes:* Serve this dish with your favorite steak. You can also add this to spinach salad to give it a different spin.

calories: 1$3, fat 13.9 g protein 3.6 g carb $.8 g fiber 1.2 g.

Pistachio-Apricot Couscous

Ingredients: *(Cook time: 1$ minutes)*

- 2 teaspoons lemon rind, finely grated
- 2 tablespoons lemon juice
- 1/4 cup fresh flat-leaf parsley leaves, finely chopped
- 1/4 cup fresh coriander leaves, finely chopped
- 1/2 cup pistachio kernels
- 1/2 cup dried apricots, thinly sliced
- 1 tablespoon olive oil
- 1 1/2 cups whole-grain couscous
- 2 cups boiling water

Methods• *(Serving: 4)*

1. Place the couscous into a large-sized heat-safe bowl. Add the boiling water, cover, and set aside for about 5 minutes, or until the couscous absorbs the water.
2. With a fork, Ouff the couscous to separate the grains.
3. Meanwhile, in a small-sized jug, whisk the oil and the lemon juice; season with the salt and pepper.

4. Add the oil mixture, apricots, pistachios, lemon rind, coriander, and parsley into the couscous; toss to combine and serve.

Per Serving:

calories: 433, fat 12.9 g, protein 12.80 g, carb 63.50 g, fiber 3.90 g.

Spicy Wilted Greens with Garlic

Ingredients: (Cook time: 5 minutes)

- 1 tablespoon olive oil
- 2 garlic cloves, minced
- 3 cups sliced greens (kale, spinach, chard, beet greens, dandelion greens, or a combination)
- Pinch salt Pinch red pepper flakes (or more to taste)

Methods: (Serving: 2)

1. Heat the olive oil in a sauté pan over medium-high heat. Add garlic and sauté for 30 seconds, or just until it's fragrant.
2. Add the greens, salt, and pepper flakes and stir to combine. Let the greens wilt, but do not overcook. Remove the pan from the heat and serve.

Per Serving:

calories: 91; fat: 7g; protein: 1g; carbs: 7g; fiber: 3g.

Roasted Broccoli with Garlic and Romano

Ingredients: (Cook time: 10 minutes)

- 1 bunch broccoli (about 5 ounces)

- 1 tablespoon olive oil
- '/2 teaspoon garlic powder
- '/4 teaspoon salt
- 2 tablespoons grated Romano cheese

Methods: (Serving: 2

1. Preheat the oven to 400°F and set the oven rack to the middle position. Line a sheet pan with parchment paper or foil.
2. Slice the tough ends off the broccoli and place in a medium bowl. Add the olive oil, garlic powder, and salt and toss to combine. Arrange broccoli on the lined sheet pan.
3. Roast for 7 minutes, flipping pieces over halfway through the roasting time.
4. Remove the pan from the oven and sprinkle the cheese over the broccoli. With a pair of tongs, carefully flip the pieces over to coat all sides.
5. Return to the oven for another 2 to 3 minutes, or until the cheese melts and starts to turn golden.

Per Serving:

calories: 114; fat: 9g; protein: 4g; carbs: $g; fiber: 2g.

White Beans with Rosemary, Sage, And Garlic

Ingredients: (Cook time: 10 minutes)

- 1 tablespoon olive oil
- 2 garlic cloves, minced
- 1 (15-ounce) can white cannellini beans, drained and rinsed
- '/4 teaspoon dried sage
- 1 teaspoon minced fresh rosemary (from 1 sprig) plus 1 whole fresh rosemary sprig
- '/2 cup low-Sodium chicken stock

- Salt

1. Heat the olive oil in a sauté pan over medium-high heat. Add the garlic and sauté for 30 seconds.
2. Add the beans, sage, minced and whole rosemary, and chicken stock and bring the mixture to a boil.
3. Reduce the heat to medium and simmer the beans for 10 minutes, or until most of the liquid is evaporated. If desired, mash some of the beans with a fork to thicken them.
4. Season with salt. Remove the rosemary sprig before serving

Per Serving:

calories: 155; fat: 7g; protein: 6g; carbs: 17g; fiber: 8g.

Moroccan-Style Couscous

Ingredients: *(Cook time: 5 minutes)*

- 1 tablespoon olive oil
- ¾ cup couscous
- ¼ teaspoon garlic powder
- ¼ teaspoon salt
- ¼ teaspoon cinnamon
- 1 cup water
- 2 tablespoons raisins
- 2 tablespoons minced dried apricots
- 2 teaspoons minced fresh parsley

Methods: *(Serving: 2)*

1. Heat the olive oil in a saucepan over medium-high heat.

2. Add the couscous, garlic powder, salt, and cinnamon. Stir for 1 minute to toast the couscous and spices.
3. Add the water, raisins, and apricots and bring the mixture to a boil.
4. Cover the pot and turn off the heat.
5. Let the couscous sit for 4 to 5 minutes and then Ouff it with a fork. Add parsley and season with additional salt or spices as needed.

Per Serving:

calories: 338; fat: 8g; protein: 9g; carbs: $9g; fiber: 4g

Red Pepper Hummus

Ingredients: (Cook time: 0 minutes)

- 6 ounces roasted red peppers, peeled and chopped
- 16 ounces canned chickpeas, drained and rinsed
- '/4 cup Greek yogurt
- 3 tablespoons tahini paste
- Juice of 1 lemon
- 3 garlic cloves, minced
- 1 tablespoon olive oil
- A pinch of salt and black pepper
- 1 tablespoon parsley, chopped

Methods• (Serving: 6)

1. In your food processor, combine the red peppers with the rest of the ingredients except the oil and the parsley and pulse well.
2. Add the oil, pulse again, divide into cups, sprinkle the parsley on top, and serve as a party spread.

Per Serving:

Calories 255; Fat 11.4 g; Protein 6.5 g Carbs 17.4 g

Sauce and Dressing

Garlic Yogurt Sauce

Ingredients: *(Cook time: 5 minutes)*

- 1 cup low-fat (2%) plain Greek yogurt
- ½ teaspoon garlic powder
- freshly squeezed lemon juice
- 1 tablespoon olive oil
- ¼ teaspoon kosher salt

Methods: *(Serving: 4)*

1. Mix all the Shopping List: in a medium bowl until well combined.
2. Spoon the yogurt sauce into a container and refrigerate.
3. Store the covered container in the refrigerator for up to 7 days.

Per Serving:

calories 75; fat: 5g; protein: 6g. carbs: 3g

Light Tartar Dill Sauce

Ingredients: *(Cook time: 0 minutes)*

- 1 1/2 tablespoons capers, minced
- 1 cup light sour cream (you can use fat free)
- 1 tablespoon fresh parsley, minced
- ½ lemon, juice
- ¼ teaspoon salt
- 2 tablespoons honey Dijon mustard
- 3 tablespoons fresh dill, minced

- Pinch pepper

Methods• (Serving: 6)

1. Mix all of the ingredients in a bowl.
2. Serve and enjoy.

Per Serving:

calories 38, [at 4.3 g protein 1.7 g carbs 3.7 g [ther 0.$ g

Tasty Tzatziki Sauce

Ingredients: (Cook time: 0 minutes)

- 2 cups plain Greek yogurt
- 1 large English cucumber, grated, with all the liquid squeezed out
- 3 tbsps. fresh dill, chopped
- 1 tsp. garlic, minced
- Pinch of sea salt

Methods• (Serving: 32 tbsp.)

1. In a medium bowl, stir together all the ingredients until well blended.
2. Store in a sealed container in the refrigerator for up to 4 days.

Per Serving:

calories: 14, fat: 1 g protein: 1 g carbs: 1 g

Simple and Easy Hummus

Ingredients: *(Cook time: 0 minutes)*

- 1 can (15 ounce) chickpeas, drained and then rinsed
- 2 garlic cloves
- 3 tablespoons tahini
- 3 tablespoons olive oil
- 2 tablespoons lemon juice
- ½ teaspoon salt

Methods: *(Serving: 4)*

1. Put all the ingredients in a food processor or a blender.
2. Process or blend until the texture is pasty.

Per Serving:

calories 548, fat 23 g, protein 22.6 g, carbs 67.5 g, fiber 19.6 g

Romesco Sauce

Ingredients: *(Cook time: 10 minutes)*

- ½ cup raw, unsalted almonds
- 4 medium garlic cloves (do not peel)
- 12-ounce jar of roasted red peppers, drained
- ½ cup canned diced fire-roasted tomatoes, drained
- 1 teaspoon smoked paprika
- ½ teaspoon kosher salt
- Pinch cayenne pepper teaspoons red wine vinegar
- 2 tablespoons olive oil

Methods: *(Serving: 1)*

1. Preheat the oven to 350°F.
2. Place the almonds and garlic cloves on a sheet pan and toast in the oven for 10 minutes. Remove from the oven and peel the garlic when cool enough to handle.
3. Place the almonds in the bowl of a food processor. Process the almonds until they resemble coarse sand, to 45 seconds.
4. Add the garlic, peppers, tomatoes, paprika, salt, and cayenne. Blend until smooth. Once the mixture is smooth, add the vinegar and oil and blend until well combined.
5. Taste and add more vinegar or salt if needed. Scoop the romesco sauce into a container and refrigerate.

Per Serving:

calories: 1$8; fat: 13g; protein: 4g; carbs: 10g

Aioli Sauce

Ingredients: (Cook time: 4 minutes)

- 1 cup olive oil
- 1 lemon, juice
- 1 whole egg
- '/z teaspoon mustard, good prepared
- '/2 teaspoon salt
- 2 large garlic cloves (or 3 medium)
- White pepper, to taste

Methods• (Serving: 1)

1. Except for the oil, put the rest of the ingredients into a food processor with the steel blade attached; process for 2 minutes at HIGH.
2. With the motor still running, pour the olive oil in the pierced food pusher. Pour in small parts if it is too small to contain all the oil at once.

3. Let the oil drip in; process 2 minutes more. Open the processor and transfer the aioli into a serving bowl.

Per Serving:

calories 4$4, fat 31.7 g protein 1.6 g carbs 0.9 g fiber 0 g

Chermoula Sauce

Ingredients: (Cook time: 10 minutes)

- 1 cup packed parsley leaves
- 1 cup cilantro leaves
- '/2 cup mint leaves
- 1 teaspoon chopped garlic
- '/2 teaspoon ground cumin
- '/2 teaspoon ground coriandcr
- '/2 teaspoon smoked paprika
- '/ teaspoon cayenne pepper
- '/ teaspoon kosher salt
- 3 tablespoons freshly squeezed lemon juice
- 3 tablespoons water
- '/2 cup extra-virgin olive oil

Methods• (Serving: 1)

1. Place all the List: in a blender or food processor and blend until smooth.
2. Pour the chermoula into a container and refrigerate.
3. Store the covered container in the refrigerator for up to 5 days.

Per Serving:

calories 257; fat: 27g; protein: 1g; carbs: 4 g

Tahini Yogurt Sauce

Ingredients: *(Cook time: 0 minutes)*

- 6 tablespoons Greek yogurt
- 2 tablespoons tahini paste
- 2 tablespoons freshly squeezed lemon juice
- 1/4 teaspoon salt
- 1 garlic clove, pressed

Methods: *(Serving: 3/4 cup)*

1. In a medium bowl, mix all the ingredients until well blended.
2. Serve as accompaniment to roasted eggplants and bell peppers. Or serve as you would any tahini.

Per Serving:

calories 271, fat 18.5 g, protein 16.3 g, carbs 12.3 g., fiber 3 g

Creamy Yogurt Citrus Dressing

Ingredients: *(Cook time: 0 minutes)*

- 1 cup plain Greek yogurt
- 1 large lemon, zested and juiced
- ½ teaspoon dried parsley
- ½ teaspoon dried oregano

- 1½ teaspoons garlic salt
- Freshly ground black pepper, to taste

Methods: (Servings: 2 cup)

1. Stir together the yogurt, lemon zest and juice, parsley, oregano, garlic salt, and pepper in a large bowl.
2. The dressing can be served with a salad or sliced vegetables of your choice.

Per Serving

calories: 135 fats: 5.8g protein: 10.8g carbs: 9.8g fiber: 1.1g

Homemade Red Wine Vinegar Dressing

Ingredients: (Cook time: 0 minutes)

- ¼ cup plus 2 tablespoons extra-virgin olive oil
- 1 tablespoon apple cider vinegar
- 2 tablespoons red wine vinegar
- 2 teaspoons Dijon mustard
- 2 teaspoons honey
- ⅛ teaspoon kosher salt
- ½ teaspoon minced garlic
- ⅛ teaspoon freshly ground black pepper

Methods: (Servings: 2 cup)

1. Whisk together the olive oil, vinegars, Dijon mustard, honey, salt, garlic, and pepper in a bowl until smooth.
2. Pour the dressing into a jar and refrigerate to chill until ready to serve.

Per Serving

Calories: 390 fats: 40g protein: <1g carbs: 5.7g fiber: 0g

Ranch-Style Cauliflower Dressing

Ingredients: *(Cook time: 0 minutes)*

- 2 cups frozen cauliflower, thawed
- ½ cup unsweetened plain almond milk
- 2 tablespoons apple cider vinegar
- 2 tablespoons extra-virgin olive oil
- 1 garlic clove, peeled
- 2 teaspoons finely chopped fresh parsley
- 2 teaspoons finely chopped scallions
- 1 teaspoon finely chopped fresh dill
- ½ teaspoon onion powder
- ½ teaspoon Dijon mustard
- ½ teaspoon salt
- ¼ teaspoon freshly ground black pepper

Methods: *(Servings: 8)*

1. Place all the ingredients in a blender and pulse until creamy and smooth.
2. Serve immediately, or transfer to an airtight container to refrigerate for up to 3 days

Per Serving:

calories: 41 fats: 3.6g protein: 1.0g carbs: 1.9g fiber: 1.1g

Avocado Dressing

Ingredients: *(Cook time: 0 minutes)*

- 1 large avocado, pitted and peeled
- ½ cup water
- 2 tbsps. tahini
- 2 tbsps. freshly squeezed lemon juice
- 1 tsp. dried basil
- 1 tsp. white wine vinegar
- 1 garlic clove
- ¼ tsp. pink Himalayan salt
- ¼ tsp. freshly ground black pepper

Methods: *(Servings: 12 tbsps.)*

1. Combine all the ingredients in a food processor and blend until smooth.

Per Serving:

calories: 38, fat: 3.5 g, protein: 1 g, carbs: 1.5 g

Orange-Garlic Dressing

Ingredients: *(Cook time: 0 minutes)*

- ¼ cup extra-virgin olive oil
- 1 orange, zested
- 2 tablespoons freshly squeezed orange juice
- ¾ teaspoon za'atar seasoning
- 1 teaspoon garlic powder
- ½ teaspoon salt
- ¼ teaspoon Dijon mustard

- Freshly ground black pepper, to taste

Methods: *(Servings: 2.)*

1. Whisk together all ingredients in a bowl until well combined.
2. Serve immediately or refrigerate until ready to serve.

Per Serving:

calories: 287 fats: 26.7g protein: 1.2g carbs: 12.0g fiber: 2.1g

Garlic Lemon-Tahini Dressing

Ingredients: *(Cook time: 0 minutes)*

- ½ cup tahini
- ¼ cup extra-virgin olive oil
- ¼ cup freshly squeezed lemon juice
- 1 garlic clove, finely minced
- 2 teaspoons salt

Methods: *(Servings: 8 to 10)*

1. In a glass mason jar with a lid, combine the tahini, olive oil, lemon juice, garlic, and salt.
2. Cover and shake well until combined and creamy.
3. Store in the refrigerator for up to 2 weeks.

Per Serving

calories: 121 fat: 12.0g protein: 2.0g carbs: 3.0g fiber: 1.0g

Creamy Cider Yogurt Dressing

Ingredients: *(Cook time: 0 minutes)*

- 1 cup plain, unsweetened, full-fat Greek yogurt
- ½ cup extra-virgin olive oil
- ½ lemon, juiced
- 1 tablespoon chopped fresh oregano
- ½ teaspoon dried parsley
- ½ teaspoon kosher salt
- ¼ teaspoon garlic powder
- ¼ teaspoon freshly ground black pepper

Methods: *(Servings: 2)*

1. In a large bowl, whisk all ingredients to combine.
2. Serve chilled or at room temperature.

Per Serving

calories: 407 fat: 40.7g protein: 8.3g carbs: 3.8g fiber: 0.5g

Lemony Tahini Dressing

Ingredients: *(Cook time: 0 minutes)*

- 2 tbsps. extra-virgin olive oil
- 2 tbsps. tahini
- Juice of ½ lemon
- 1 clove garlic, crushed
- 1 tsp. honey ¼ tsp. Himalayan salt

Methods: *(Servings: ½ cup)*

1. Whisk together the tahini, olive oil, lemon juice, garlic, honey, and salt in a small bowl.
2. Give it a stir right before serving.

Per Serving:

calories: 112, fat: 11 g, protein: 1 g, carbs: 4 g

Balsamic Dressing

Ingredients: *(Cook time: 0 minutes)*

- 2 tbsps. Dijon mustard
- ¼ cup balsamic vinegar
- ¾ cup olive oil

Methods: *(Servings: 1 cup)*

1. Put all ingredients in a jar with a tight-fitting lid.
2. Put on the lid and shake vigorously until thoroughly combined.
3. Refrigerate until ready to use and shake well before serving.

Per Serving:

Calories: 189, Fat: 21.1 g, Protein: 0.3 g, Carbs: 0.6 g

Lime-Cilantro Dressing

Ingredients: *(Cook time: 0 minutes)*

- ¼ cup extra-virgin olive oil
- ¾ cup 2% Greek yogurt
- Juice of 1 lime

- 1 small bunch cilantro
- 1 garlic clove
- 2 tbsps. honey
- '/4 tsp. sea salt

Methods• (SCrvings: 1!/8 cups):

1. In a food processor or high-speed blender, add all the ingredients and blend until smooth.
2. The dressing can be stored in the refrigerator for up to a week in an airtight container.

Per Serving:

Calories 96; fat: 7g; Protein: 2g. Carbs: 6g

Snacks and Appetizer

Baked Cashews with Rosemary

Ingredients: *(Cook time: 3 minutes)*

- 2 cups roasted and unsalted whole cashews
- 1 tsp. olive oil
- 2 sprigs of fresh rosemary (1 chopped and 1 whole)
- 1 tsp. kosher salt
- ½ tsp. honey

Methods: *(Servings: 2 cups)*

1. Preheat the air fryer to 300ºF.
2. In a medium bowl, whisk together the chopped rosemary, olive oil, kosher salt, and honey. Set aside.
3. Spray the air fryer basket with cooking spray, then place the cashews and the whole rosemary sprig in the basket and bake for 3 minutes.
4. Remove the cashews and rosemary from the air fryer, then discard the rosemary and add the cashews to the olive oil mixture, tossing to coat.
5. Allow to cool for 15 minutes before serving.

Per Serving:

calories: 180, fat: 15 g, protein: 5 g, carbs: 8 g, fiber: 1 g

Spicy Broccoli Poppers

Ingredients: *(Cook time: 10 minutes)*

- 1-pound broccoli, cut into small florets
- 2 tbsps. plain yogurt

- 2 tbsps. chickpea flour
- '/2 tsp. red chili powder
- '/4 tsp. ground cumin
- '/4 tsp. ground turmeric
- Salt, to taste

Methods• *(Servings: 4)*

1. Preheat the Air fryer to 400°F and grease an Air fryer basket.
2. Mix together the yogurt, red chili powder, cumin, turmeric and salt in a bowl until well combined.
3. Stir in the broccoli and generously coat with marinade. Refrigerate for about 30 minutes and sprinkle the broccoli Oorets with chickpea Oour.
4. Arrange the broccoli florets in the Air fryer basket and air fry for about 10 minutes, flipping once in between. Dish out and serve warm.

Per Serving:

calories: 69, fat: 1 g protein: 3 g carbs: 13 g fiber: $ g

Paprika Tiger Shrimp

Ingredients: *(Cook time: 10 minutes)*

- 2 tbsps. olive oil
- 1-pound tiger shrimp
- '/2 tsp. smoked paprika
- Salt, to taste

Methods• *(Servings: 2)*

1. Preheat the Air fryer to 390°F and grease an Air fryer basket.
2. Mix all the ingredients in a large bowl until well combined.
3. Place the shrimp in the Air fryer basket and air fry for about 10 minutes.

4. Dish out and serve warm.

Per Serving:

calories: 213, fat: 11 g protein: 25 g carbs: 0 g fiber: 0 g

Herbed Pita Chips

Ingredients: *(Cook time: $ to 6 minutes)*

- 2 whole grain
- 6-inch pitas

- '/4 tsp. dried basil
- '/4 tsp. marjoram
- Cooking spray
- '/4 tsp. ground oregano
- '/4 tsp. garlic powder
- '/4 tsp. ground thyme
- '/4 tsp. Salt

Methods• (Servings: 4)

1. Preheat the air fryer to 330°F. Mix all the seasonings together. Cut each pita half into 4 wedges. Break apart wedges at the fold.
2. Mist one side of pita wedges with oil. Sprinkle with half of seasoning mix. Turn pita wedges over, mist the other side with oil, and sprinkle with remaining seasonings.
3. Place pita wedges in air fryer basket and bake for 2 minutes.
4. Shake the basket and bake for 2 minutes longer. Shake again, and if needed, bake for 1 or 2 more minutes, or until crisp.
5. Watch carefully because at this point they will cook very quickly. Serve hot.

Per Servings

calories: 70, fat: 1 g, protein: 2 g, carbs: 14 g, fiber: 2 g,

Tasty Fish Nuggets

Ingredients: (Cook time: 10 minutes)

- 2 tbsps. olive oil
- 1-pound cod, cut into 1x2½-inch strips
- 2 eggs
- 1 cup whole wheat flour
- ¾ cup breadcrumbs
- Pinch of salt

Methods: (Servings: 4)

1. Preheat the Air fryer to 380ºF and grease an Air fryer basket.
2. Place flour in a shallow dish and whisk the eggs in a second dish. Mix breadcrumbs, salt and oil in a third shallow dish.
3. Coat the fish strips evenly in flour and dip in the egg. Roll into the breadcrumbs evenly and arrange the nuggets in the Air fryer basket.
4. Air fry for about 10 minutes and dish out to serve warm.

Per Serving:

calories: 404, fat: 11.6 g, protein: 34.6 g, carbs: 36.8 g, fiber: 0 g

Golden Avocado Fries

Ingredients: (Cook time: 7 minutes)

- 1 avocado, peeled, pitted and sliced into 8 pieces
- 1 egg

- '/2 cup panko breadcrumbs
- '/4 cup whole wheat flour
- 1 tsp. water Salt and black pepper, to taste

Methods• (Servings: 2)

1. Preheat the Air fryer to 400°F and grease an Air fryer basket.
2. Place Oour, salt and black pepper in a shallow dish and whisk the egg with water in a second dish.
3. Place the breadcrumbs in a third shallow dish.
4. Coat the avocado slices evenly in flour and dip in the egg mixture. Roll into the breadcrumbs evenly and arrange the avocado slices in the Air fryer basket.
5. Air fry for about 7 minutes, flipping once in between and dish out to serve warm.

Per Serving:

calories: 363, fat: 22.4 g protein: 8.3 g carbs: 3$.7 g fiber: 2 g

Crispy Zucchini Fries

Ingredients: (Cook time: 10 minutes)

- 2 tbsps. olive oil
- 1-pound zucchini, sliced into 2'/2-inch sticks
- '/4 cup panko breadcrumbs
- Salt, to taste

Methods• (Servings: 4)

1. Preheat the Air fryer to 425°F and grease an Air fryer basket
2. Season zucchini with salt and keep aside for about 10 minutes.
3. Place breadcrumbs in a shallow dish and coat zucchini fries in it.
4. Arrange the zucchini fries in the Air fryer basket and air fry for about 10 minutes.
5. Dish out and serve warm.

Per Serving:

calories: 158, fat: 8.3 g, protein: 4.1 g, carbs: 18.4 g, fiber: 4 g

Savory Pistachio Balls

Ingredients: *(Cook time: 5 minutes)*

- ½ cup pistachios, unsalted
- 1 cup dates, pitted
- ½ tsp. ground fennel seeds
- ½ cup raisins
- Pinch of pepper

Methods: *(Servings: 16)*

1. Add all ingredients into the food processor and process until well combined.
2. Make small balls and place onto the baking tray and place in the refrigerator for 1 hour.
3. Serve and enjoy.

Per Serving:

calories 55, protein 0.8g, fat 0.9g, carbs 12.5g

Avocado Chickpea Delight on Toast

Ingredients: *(Cook time: 5 minutes)*

- 4 slices Whole-grain bread
- 1 Ripe avocado
- 1 cup Cooked chickpeas

- 1 clove Garlic, minced
- Lemon juice from half a lemon
- 1 tablespoon Olive oil
- Salt and pepper: to taste
- A pinch Chili flakes: (optional)
- Fresh parsley, finely chopped: for garnish

Methods• (Servings: 4)

1. Begin by toasting your whole-grain bread slices until they achieve a golden, crispy texture.
2. In a mixing bowl, mash the ripe avocado using a fork until it reaches a smooth consistency.
3. Season the mashed avocado with minced garlic, lemon juice, olive oil, salt, pepper, and if desired, a hint of chili flakes. Stir these ingredients together to combine them evenly.
4. Spread the seasoned avocado mixture generously on each slice of toasted bread.
5. Carefully place whole cooked chickpeas on top of the avocado spread, distributing them evenly across the toast.
6. As a final touch, garnish each slice of toast with finely chopped fresh parsley, adding both flavor and a burst of color.

Per Serving:

calories: 2$0, fat: 14g protein: 7g carbs: 24g

Crispy Chickpea Falafel with Creamy Yogurt Dip

Ingredients: (Cook time: 13 minutes)

- 1 cup canned chickpeas, drained and rinsed
- 1 small onion, chopped
- 2 cloves garlic, minced

- 1/2 cup fresh parsley, chopped
- 1 teaspoon ground cumin
- 1 teaspoon ground coriander
- Salt and pepper: to taste
- 2 tablespoons olive oil
- 1 cup plain yogurt
- 1 garlic clove, minced
- 1 teaspoon lemon juice

Methods• (Servings: 4)

1. In a food processor, blend together chickpeas, chopped onion, minced garlic, chopped parsley, cumin, coriander, salt, and pepper. Pulse until you achieve a coarsely ground mixture.
2. Take small amounts of the chickpea mixture and roll them into bite-sized falafel balls.
3. In a skillet, warm the olive oil over medium Oame.
4. Fry the falafel balls in batches, turning them occasionally for an even golden color on all sides. 5. Once fried, transfer the falafels to a plate lined with paper towels to absorb excess oil.
5. For the yogurt sauce, whisk together plain yogurt, minced garlic, lemon juice, and a pinch of salt in a bowl until smooth.
6. Serve the falafels on a serving dish with the creamy yogurt sauce as a dip. Optionally, stuff the falafels and yogurt sauce in pita pockets for a delightful snack.

Per Serving:

calories: 220, fat: 9g protein: 9g. carbs: 23g

Rosemary and Sea Salt Infused Roasted Almonds

Ingredients: *(Cook time: 15 minutes)*

- 2 cups raw almonds
- 1 tablespoon olive oil
- 2 teaspoons fresh rosemary, finely chopped
- 1 teaspoon sea salt

Methods: *(Servings: 4)*

1. Heat your oven to 350°F. Place the almonds on a baking tray in a single layer.
2. Evenly sprinkle the olive oil over the almonds, ensuring they are well coated.
3. Scatter the chopped rosemary and sea salt over the almonds. Gently mix to ensure the almonds are uniformly covered with rosemary and sea salt.
4. Bake for 10-15 minutes, giving them a stir midway, until the almonds turn a rich golden hue and exude a delightful aroma.
5. Once done, take out from the oven and set aside to cool. Serve as a fragrant, flavorful snack.

Per Serving:

calories: 200, fat: 18g, protein: 6g, carbs: 6g

Caper and Sardine Toasts

Ingredients: *(Cook time: 10 minutes)*

- 1 sliced baguette, into 1-inch rounds
- 1 can (4 oz.), sardines in olive oil, drained
- 2 tablespoons capers
- 1 clove garlic, minced
- 1 small finely chopped red onion

- Lemon juice: from 1 lemon
- 1 tablespoon olive oil
- Salt and pepper: to taste
- Fresh parsley leaves: for garnish

Methods• (Servings: 4)

1. Heat your oven to 350°F in preparation. Arrange the slices of baguette on a baking sheet and bake them for about 5-7 minutes until they become crispy.
2. In a mixing bowl, blend together the sardines, capers, minced garlic, red onion, lemon juice, and olive oil. Use a fork to mix and mash the ingredients.
3. Taste and adjust the Oavoring with salt and pepper as needed. Once the baguette slices are adequately toasted, take them out of the oven.
4. Top each slice of toasted baguette with the sardine and caper mixture.
5. Finalize with a garnish of fresh parsley leaves, a few whole sardines, and capers on each toast before serving.

Per Serving:

calories: 220, fat: J2g protein: 10g carbs: 18g

Fruit, Veggie, and Cheese Board

Ingredients: (Cook time: 0 minutes)

- 2 cups sliced fruits, *(apples, pears, plums, or peaches)*
- 2 cups finger-food fruits, *(berries, cherries, grapes, or figs)*
- 2 cups raw vegetables cut into sticks, *(carrots, celery, broccoli, cauliflower, or whole cherry tomatoes)*
- 1 cup cured, canned, or jarred vegetables, *(roasted peppers or artichoke hearts, or 1/2 cup olives)*
- 1 cup cubed cheese, *(goal cheese, Gorgonzola, feta, Manchego, or Asiago)*

1. Wash all the fresh produce and cut into slices or bite-size pieces, as described in the ingredients list.
2. Arrange all the ingredients on a wooden board or serving tray.
3. Include small spoons for items like the berries and olives, and a fork or knife for the cheeses. Serve with small plates and napkins

Per Serving

calories: 213; fat: 9g; carbs: 3Og; protein: 6g; fiber: $g

Lemony Garlic Hummus

Ingredients: *(Cook time: 0 minutes)*

- 1 (15-ounce) can chickpeas, drained, liquid reserved
- 3 tablespoons freshly squeezed lemon juice
- 2 tablespoons peanut butter
- 3 tablespoons extra-virgin olive oil, divided
- 2 garlic cloves
- '/4 teaspoon kosher or sea salt (optional)
- Raw veggies or whole-grain crackers, for serving (optional)

Methods• (Servings: 6)

1. In the bowl of a food processor, combine the chickpeas and 2 tablespoons of the reserved chickpea liquid with the lemon juice, peanut butter, 2 tablespoons of oil, and the garlic.
2. Process the mixture for 1 minute. Scrape down the sides of the bowl with a rubber spatula. Process for 1 more minute, or until smooth.
3. Put in a serving bowl, drizzle with the remaining 1 tablespoon of olive oil, sprinkle with the salt, if using, and serve with veggies or crackers, if desired.

calories: 165; fat: 11g; protein: 5g; carbs: 14g; fiber: 4g

Grilled Polenta Vegetables Bites

Ingredients: (*Cook time: 15 minutes*)

- 1 1/2 to 2 tablespoons olive oil
- 1 green bell pepper, chopped
- 1 tomato sliced
- 1 tube (18-ounce) Polenta, pre-cooked
- 1/2 teaspoon garlic powder
- 1/2 yellow onion, chopped into big chunks
- 2 jalapenos, sliced, de-seeded
- 2-3 slices Swiss cheese or your cheese of choice
- 5-6 pieces' baby Bella mushrooms

Optional:

- Chopped parsley and black olives
- Salt and pepper, to taste

Methods: (*Servings: 6-8*)

1. Preheat the grill. Meanwhile, slice the polenta into 1/4-1/2 slices. Brush both sides with the olive oil and set aside.
2. Place the chopped vegetables into a mixing bowl, add the garlic, remaining oil, and season with salt and pepper to taste; toss lightly.
3. Grill the polenta and the vegetables for about 15 to 20 minutes, turning at least once, until lightly browned.
4. Remove from the grill and assemble the sandwiches with cheese, vegetables, and tomato slice.

5. Top with the olives and parsley, if desired. Secure with toothpicks.

Per Serving:

calories 1$O, fat 11 g protein 6 g carbs 16 g fiber 2 g.

Polenta Pizza Bites

Ingredients: *(Cook time: $ minutes)*

- 1 tube polenta, cut into 1/2-inch slices
- 1/2 cup pizza sauce
- 1/2 cup mozzarella cheese
- For the toppings:
- Bell peppers, sliced
- Basil, minced
- Mushrooms, chopped
- Black olives, chopped

Methods• *(Servings: 12*

1. Preheat the broiler of the oven. Line a baking sheet with parchment paper; grease the paper lightly with olive oil spray.
2. Place the polenta slices on the baking sheet; broil for about 2 minutes.
3. Spread pizza sauce over each polenta, top with cheese, and your preferred toppings.
4. Broil for another 2 minutes, or until the cheese melts to your liking.

Per Serving:

calories 163, fat 1.7 g barbs 32.3 g [ther 1.4 g protein 4.6 g.

Carrot Dip

Ingredients: *(Cook time: 12 minutes)*

- 1 piece (2 inches) fresh ginger root, peeled, thinly sliced
- 1½ teaspoons ground coriander
- 1 pound carrots, peeled, thinly sliced
- 1/3 cup apricot preserves
- 1/8 teaspoon cayenne pepper
- 2 tablespoons fresh lemon juice
- 3 cloves garlic, thinly sliced
- ¾ teaspoon salt, divided
- 4 teaspoons toasted sesame oil
- 2 cups water

Methods: *(Servings: 10)*

1. Place the carrots, ginger, garlic, and ¼ teaspoon salt in a large-sized saucepan. Add the water, cover, and bring to a boil.
2. When boiling, reduce the heat, simmer covered for about 10-12 minutes, or until the carrots are drained. Drain.
3. Transfer the carrots to a food processor. Add the remaining 1/2 teaspoon salt and the rest of the ingredients; process until the mixture is smooth.

Per Serving:

calories 65, fat 2.1 g, protein 6 g, carbs 12.1 g, fiber 1.5 g.

Zucchini Pizza Rolls

Ingredients: *(Cook time: 12 minutes)*

Makes: 24 rolls Prep: less than 15 min

- 4 large zucchinis, sliced lengthwise into 1/4-inch thick slices
- 1/2 cup sun-dried tomatoes, chopped
- 1/2 cup black olives, chopped
- 1 tablespoon olive oil
- 1 cup pizza sauce
- Freshly ground black pepper
- Red pepper flakes (optional)
- Sea salt

Methods• *(Servings: 4 24 rolls])*

1. Preheat a grill or a broiler.
2. Brush each slice of zucchini lightly with the olive oil and season with salt and pepper; grill or broil for about 2 minutes each side, or until softened. Let cool slightly.
3. On 1/2 side of the zucchini slices, spread a thin layer of pizza sauce. Sprinkle the olives, sun-dried tomato, and if using, red pepper flakes over the sauce.
4. Starting on the end with the pizza sauce, roll each slice. If necessary, secure with toothpicks.

Per Serving:

calories 20, [at 1 g protein   1 g carbs 2 g [ther <1 g.

Dessert and Sweet

Tasty Black Forest Pies

Ingredients: *(Cook time: 15 minutes)*

- 1 (10-by-15-inch) sheet frozen puff pastry, thawed
- 1 egg white, beaten
- 3 tbsps. milk or dark chocolate chips
- 2 tbsps. thick, hot fudge sauce
- 2 tbsps. chopped dried cherries
- 2 tbsps. coconut sugar
- ½ tsp. cinnamon

Methods: *(Servings: 6)*

1. Preheat the air fryer to 350ºF (177ºC).
2. In a small bowl, combine the chocolate chips, fudge sauce, and dried cherries. Roll out the puff pastry on a floured surface.
3. Cut into 6 squares with a sharp knife. Divide the chocolate chip mixture into the center of each puff pastry square. Fold the squares in half to make triangles. Firmly press the edges with the tines of a fork to seal.
4. Brush the triangles on all sides sparingly with the beaten egg white. Sprinkle the tops with sugar and cinnamon.
5. Put in the air fryer basket and bake for 15 minutes or until the triangles are golden brown. The filling will be hot, so cool for at least 20 minutes before serving.

Per Serving:

Calories: 223, Fat: 12 g, Protein: 3 g, Carbs: 25 g, Fiber: 2 g

Dark Chocolate Cake

Ingredients: *(Cook time: 10 minutes)*

- 2 eggs
- 3½ oz. peanut butter
- 3½ oz. sugar free dark chocolate, chopped
- 1½ tbsps. almond flour
- 3½ tbsps. swerve

Methods: *(Servings: 4)*

1. Preheat the Air fryer to 375ºF and grease 4 regular sized ramekins.
2. Microwave all chocolate bits with peanut butter in a bowl for about 3 minutes.
3. Remove from the microwave and whisk in the eggs and swerve. Stir in the flour and mix well until smooth.
4. Transfer the mixture into the ramekins and arrange in the Air fryer basket.
5. Bake for about 10 minutes and dish out to serve.

Per Serving:

calories: 379, fat: 29.7 g, protein: 5.2 g, carbs: 4 g, fiber: 0 g

Healthy Fruit Muffins

Ingredients: *(Cook time: 10 minutes)*

- 1 banana, peeled and chopped
- 1 apple, peeled, cored and chopped
- 1 cup low-fat milk
- 1 pack Oreo biscuits, crushed
- 1 tsp. cocoa powder
- 1 tsp. fresh lemon juice

- 1 tsp. honey
- '/4 tsp. baking soda
- '/4 tsp. baking powder Pinch of ground cinnamon

Methods• (Servings: 6)

1. Preheat the Air fryer to 320°F (160°C) and grease 6 muffin cups lightly.
2. Mix milk, biscuits, cocoa powder, baking soda and baking powder in a bowl until a smooth mixture is formed.
3. Divide this mixture into the prepared muffin cups and transfer into the Air fryer basket. Bake for about 10 minutes and remove from Air fryer.
4. Mix banana, apple, honey, lemon juice and cinnamon in a bowl.
5. Scoop out some portion from center of muffins and Uh with the fruit mixture.
6. Refrigerate for 2 hours and serve chilled.

Per Serving:

calories: 52,Jat: 5.2 g *protein: 3.3 g carbs:* 24.5 g Jitter: *3 g*

Banana Shake Bowls

Ingredients: (Cook time: 0 minutes)

- 4 medium bananas, peeled
- 1 avocado, peeled, pitted and mashed
- ^{3}/4cup almond milk
- '/2 teaspoon vanilla extract

Methods• (Servings: 6)

1. In a blender, combine the bananas with the avocado and the other ingredients, pulse or blend all.
2. Divide into bowls and keep in the fridge until serving.

Per Serving:

calories 185, fat 4.3g, protein 6.45g, carbs 6g, fiber 4g

Rhubarb and Apples Cream

Ingredients: *(Cook time: 0 minutes)*

- 3 cups rhubarb, chopped
- 1 and ½ cups stevia
- 2 eggs, whisked
- ½ teaspoon nutmeg, ground
- 1 tablespoon avocado oil
- 1/3 cup almond milk

Methods: *(Servings: 6)*

1. In a blender, combine the rhubarb with the stevia and the rest of the ingredients, pulse well,
2. Divide into cups and serve cold.

Per Servings:

calories 200, fat 5.2g, protein 2.5g, carbs 7.6g, fiber 3.4g

Blueberries Stew

Ingredients: *(Cook time: 10 minutes)*

- 2 cups blueberries
- 3 tablespoons stevia
- 1 and ½ cups pure apple juice

- 1 teaspoon vanilla extract

1. In a pan, combine the blueberries with stevia and the other ingredients.
2. Bring to a simmer and cook over medium-low heat for 10 minutes.
3. Divide into cups and serve cold.

Per Serving:

calories 192, fat 3.4g protein 4.$g carbs 9.4g fiber 3.4g

Pumpkin Cream

Ingredients: (Cook time: $ minutes)

- 2 cups canned pumpkin Oesh
- 2 tablespoons stevia
- 1 teaspoon vanilla extract
- 2 tablespoons water
- A pinch of pumpkin spice

Methods• (Servings: 2)

1. In a pan, combine the pumpkin flesh with the other ingredients, simmer for 5 minutes.
2. Divide into cups and serve cold.

Per Servings

calories 192,Jat3.4g, protein 3.3g carbs 7.6g fiber 4.3g

Chia and Berries Smoothie Bowl

Ingredients: *(Cook time: 0 minutes)*

- 1 and ½ cup almond milk
- 1 cup blackberries
- ¼ cup strawberries, chopped
- 1 and ½ tablespoons chia seeds
- 1 teaspoon cinnamon powder

Methods: *(Servings: 2)*

1. In a blender, combine the blackberries with the strawberries and the rest of the ingredients.
2. Pulse well, and divide into small bowls and serve cold.

Per Serving:

calories 182, fat 3.4g, protein 3g, carbs 8.4g, fiber 3.4g

Minty Coconut Cream

Ingredients: *(Cook time: 0 minutes)*

- 1 banana, peeled
- 2 cups coconut flesh, shredded
- 3 tablespoons mint, chopped
- 1 and ½ cups coconut water
- 2 tablespoons stevia
- ½ avocado, pitted and peeled

Methods: *(Servings: 2)*

1. In a blender, combine the coconut with the banana and the rest of the ingredients.
2. pulse well, and divide into cups and serve cold.

Per Serving:

calories 193, fat 3.4g protein 3g carbs 7.6g fiber 3.4g

Watermelon Cream

Ingredients: *(Cook time: 0 minutes)*

- 1-pound watermelon, peeled and chopped
- 1 teaspoon vanilla extract
- 1 cup heavy cream
- 1 teaspoon lime juice
- 2 tablespoons stevia

Methods• *(Servings: 2)*

1. In a blender, combine the watermelon with the cream and the rest of the ingredients.
2. pulse well, and divide into cups and keep in the fridge for 15 minutes before serving.

Per Serving:

calories 122, fat $.7g protein 0.4g carbs 5.3gJiher 3.2g

Grapes Stew

Ingredients: *(Cook time: 10 minutes)*

- 2/3 cup stevia
- 1 tablespoon olive oil
- 1/3 cup coconut water
- 1 teaspoon vanilla extract
- 1 teaspoon lemon zest, grated
- 2 cup red grapes, halved

Methods• (Servings: 4)

1. Heat up a pan with the water over medium heat, add the oil, stevia and the rest of the ingredients.
2. Toss, simmer for 10 minutes, divide into cups and serve.

Per Servings

calories 122, fat 3.7g protein 0.4g carbs 2.3g fiber 1.2g

Papaya Cream

Ingredients: (Cook time: 0 minutes)

- 1 cup papaya, peeled and chopped
- 1 cup heavy cream
- 1 tablespoon stevia
- '/2 teaspoon vanilla extract

Methods• (Servings: 2)

1. In a blender, combine the cream with the papaya and the other ingredients.
2. Pulse well, and divide into cups and serve cold.

Per Serving:

calories 182, fat 3.1g protein 2g carbs 3.3g fiber 2.3g

Cocoa and Pears Cream

Ingredients: *(Cook time: 0 minutes)*

- 2 cups heavy creamy
- 1/3 cup stevia
- ¾ cup cocoa powder
- 6 ounces' dark chocolate, chopped
- Zest of 1 lemon
- 2 pears, chopped

Methods: *(Servings: 4)*

1. In a blender, combine the cream with the stevia and the rest of the ingredients.
2. Pulse well, and divide into cups and serve cold.

Per Serving:

calories 172, fat 5.6g, protein 4g, carbs 7.6g, fiber 3.5g

Almond Peaches Mix

Ingredients: *(Cook time: 10 minutes)*

- 1/3 cup almonds, toasted
- 1/3 cup pistachios, toasted
- 1 teaspoon mint, chopped
- ½ cup coconut water
- 1 teaspoon lemon zest, grated
- 4 peaches, halved
- 2 tablespoons stevia

Methods: (Servings: 4)

1. In a pan, combine the peaches with the stevia and the rest of the ingredients, simmer over medium heat for 10 minutes.
2. Divide into bowls and serve cold.

Per Serving:

calories 135, fat 4.1g, protein 2.3g, carbs 4.1g, fiber 3.8g

Cinnamon Banana and Semolina Pudding

Ingredients: (Cook time: 7 minutes)

- 2 cups semolina, ground
- 1 cup olive oil
- 4 cups hot water
- 2 bananas, peeled and chopped
- 1 teaspoon cinnamon powder
- 4 tablespoons stevia

Methods: (Servings: 6)

1. Heat up a pan with the oil over medium high heat, add the semolina and brown it for 3 minutes stirring often.
2. Add the water and the rest of the ingredients except the cinnamon, stir, and simmer for 4 minutes more.
3. Divide into bowls, sprinkle the cinnamon on top and serve.

Per Serving:

calories 162, fat 8g, protein 8.4g, carbs 4.3g, fiber 4.2g

Cocoa Yogurt Mix

Ingredients: *(Cook time: 0 minutes)*

- 1 tablespoon cocoa powder
- ¼ cup strawberries, chopped
- ¾ cup Greek yogurt
- 5 drops vanilla stevia

Methods: *(Servings: 2)*

1. In a bowl, mix the yogurt with the cocoa, strawberries and the stevia and whisk well.
2. Divide the mix into bowls and serve.

Per Serving:

calories 200, fat 8g, protein 4.3g, carbs 7.6g, fiber 3.4g

Minty Orange Greek Yogurt

Ingredients: *(Cook time: 0 minutes)*

- 6 tablespoons Greek yogurt, fat-free
- 4 fresh mint leaves, thinly sliced
- 1 large orange, peeled, quartered, and then sliced crosswise
- 1 1/2 teaspoons honey

Methods: *(Serving: 1)*

1. Stir together the honey and the yogurt.
2. Place the orange slices into a dessert glass.
3. Spoon the honeyed yogurt over the orange slices in the glass and scatter the mint on top of the yogurt.

Per Serving:

calories 171, protein 11 g, carbs 34 g, fiber 5 g

Orange Olive Oil Mug Cakes

Ingredients: *(Cook time: 2 minutes)*

- 6 tablespoons flour
- 2 tablespoons sugar
- ½ teaspoon baking powder
- Pinch salt
- 1 teaspoon orange zest
- 1 egg
- 2 tablespoons olive oil
- 2 tablespoons freshly squeezed orange juice
- 2 tablespoons milk
- ½ teaspoon orange extract
- ½ teaspoon vanilla extract

Methods: *(Servings: 2)*

1. In a small bowl, combine the flour, sugar, baking powder, salt, and orange zest.
2. In a separate bowl, whisk together the egg, olive oil, orange juice, milk, orange extract, and vanilla extract.
3. Pour the dry ingredients into the wet ingredients and stir to combine. The batter will be thick.
4. Divide the mixture into two small mugs that hold at least 6 ounces each, or one 12-ounce mug.
5. Microwave each mug separately. The small ones should take about 60 seconds, and one large mug should take about 90 seconds, but microwaves can vary.
6. The cake will be done when it pulls away from the sides of the mug.

Per Serving:

calories: 302; fat: 17g; protein: 6g; carbs: 33g; fiber: 1g

Conclusion

Having a busy life is surely not helpful when it comes to health and diet, but not all is lost. You don't need to starve yourself or go through painful days if you embrace the Mediterranean diet as a way of living. The Mediterranean diet is not only easy to follow, but also packed with fresh flavors and tastes, vitamins and minerals, spices and herbs, all of them being easy to incorporate into your daily cooking.

Mediterranean recipes focus on the natural taste of ingredients, combining them in an original yet classical way. The final taste is the highlight of the Mediterranean cooking, although the way the food looks is just as important and the time spent in the kitchen is crucial. Everything is reduced to the simplest of the techniques, the easiest of the ways, the tastiest of the Oavor combinations.

Therefore! Mediterranean diet cookbook made simple got you covered. A perfect collection for people that runs busy schedules. It contains recipes collection full of simple and delicious recipes that can be prepare within 15 minutes or less. All these recipes great taste, divine flavor and you will definitely be impressed with the textures and flavors. How great does that sound?! It's the perfect diet for the heart, but also for an enjoyable lifestyle without the chore of a diet!

Appendix 1

Conversions & Equivalents

Volume Equivalents (Liquid)

VS Standard		Metric (approximate)
'/4 cup	2/. oz.	60 mL
½ cup	4 fl. oz.	120 mL
1 cup	8 fl. oz.	240 mL
1½ cups	12 fl. oz.	355 mL
2 cups or 1 pint	16 fl. oz.	475 mL
4 cups or 1 quart	32 fl. oz.	1 L
1@AÚOh	128 fl. oz.	4 L

Oven Temperatures

300°F	1S0°C
325°F	165°C
350°F	180°C
375°F	190°C
400°F	200°C
425°F	220°C
4S0°6	2J0°C

Volume Equivalents (Dry)

	Metric (approximate)
'/4 teaspoon	1 mL
½ teaspoon	2 mL
*/4 teaspoon	4 mL
1 teaspoon	S mL
1 tablespoon	1$ mL

¼ cup	59 mL
⅓ cup	79 mL
½ cup	118 mL
⅔ cup	136 mL
¾ cup	177 mL
1 cup	235 mL
2 cups or 1 pint	475 mL
3 cups	700 mL
4 cups or 1 quart	1 L

Weight Equivalents

	Metric (approximate)

2 ounces	60 g
4 ounces	115 g
8 ounces	225 g
12 ounces	340 g
16 ounces or 1 pound	455 g

Appendix 2: Recipe Index

Broccoli and Carrot Pasta Salad	*$0*
Brown Rice and Chili Shrimp Bowl	*64*
Brown Rice Fritters	*63*
Brown Rice Pilaf with Pistachios and Raisins	*36*
Butternut Noodles with Mushrooms	*79*
Caper and Sardine Toasts	177
Carrot Dip	181
Cauliflower & Tomato Salad	*146*
Cauliflower Hash with Carrots	*80*
Cauliflower with Sweet Potato	*74*
Cheesy Roasted Broccolini	*149*
Chermoula Sauce	*161*
Chia and Berries Smoothie Bowl	*188*
Chicken and Olives	*113*
Chicken and Orzo Soup	*88*
Chicken Salad and Mustard Dressing	*114*
Chicken Wrap	*113*
Chickpea Salad	144
Chili Halloumi Cheese with Rice	*39*
Chili Watermelon Soup	*92*
Chunky fish soup	*84*
Cinnamon Banana and Semolina Pudding	*193*
Cinnamon Oatmeal with Dried Cranberries	*36*

Citrus Pistachios and Asparagus	71
Classic Fajita Chicken Strips	124
Cocoa and Pears Cream	191
Cocoa Yogurt Mix	193
Corn and Shrimp Salad	147
Couscous Salad	143
Cranberry and Almond Quinoa	$8
Creamy Breakfast Bulgur with Berries	37
Creamy Cider Yogurt Dressing	166
Creamy Salmon Soup	95
Creamy Tomato Hummus Soup	85
Creamy Yogurt Citrus Dressing	162
Crispy Beef Schnitzel	130
Crispy Chickpea Falafel with Creamy Yogurt Dip	lis
Crispy Potatoes	68
Crispy Sardines	106
Crispy Zucchini Fries	1r3
Cucumber Gazpacho	149
Cumin Quinoa Pilaf	60
Dark Chocolate Cake	18$
Egg-Feta Scramble	39
Fennel Bruschetta	35
Fettuccine with Spinach and Shrimp	108

Appendix 3: References

Altomare, R, et al. "The Mediterranean Diet: A History of Health." Iranian Journal of Public Health 42, no. 5 (2013): 449-45.

Billingsley, H. E., et al. "The Antioxidant Potential of the Mediterranean Diet in Patients at High Cardiovascular Risk: An In-Depth Review of the PREDIMED." Nutrition & Diabetes 8, no. 1 (2018): 13 doi:10.1038/s41387-018-0025-1.

Hibbeln, J. R, J. M. Davis, C. Steer, P. Emmett, I. Rogers, C. Williams, and J. Golding. "Maternal Seafood Consumption in Pregnancy and Neurodevelopmental Outcomes in Childhood (ALSPAC Study): An Observational Cohort Study." The Lancet 369, no. 9561 (2007): 578-855 doi:10.1016/50140-6736(07)60277-3.

International Pasta Organisation. The Truth About Pasta. Boston: Oldways Preservation Trust, 2016. Accessed June 15, 2018. https://oldwayspt.org/system/files/atoms/files/TruthAboutPasta16.pdf.

Luciano, M., et al. "Mediterranean-Type Diet and Brain Structural Change from 73 to 76 Years in a Scottish Cohort." Neurology 88, no. 5 January 31, 2017): 229-455 doi.10.1212/WNL.0000000000003559.

Mozaffarian, D., and E. B. Rimm. "Fish Intake, Contaminants, and Human Health: Evaluating the Risks and the Benefits."Journal of the American Medical Association 296, no. 15 (November 2006):1885—1899 doi:10.1001/jama.296.15.1885.

Oldways. "Oldways Mediterranean Diet Pyramid." Accessed June 20, 2018. https://oldwayspt.org/resources/oldways-mediterranean-diet-pyramid.

Pizzino, G., Irrera, N., Cucinotta, M., Pallio, G., Mannino, F., Arcoraci, V., Squadrito, F., Altavilla, D., & Bitto, A. (2017). Oxidative Stress: Harms and Benefits for Human Health. Oxidative medicine and cellular longevity, 2017, 8416763. https://doi.org/10.1155/2017/8416763

Tan, Z. S., et al. "Red Blood Cell Omega-3 Fatty Acid Levels and Markers of Accelerated Brain Aging." Neurology 78, no. 9 (February 28, 2012): 658-664 doi:10.1212/WNL.0b013e318249f6a9.

Trichopoulou, A., Martinez-Gonzalez, M. A., Tong, T. Y., Forouhi, N. G., Khandelwal, S., Prabhakaran, D., Mozaffarian, D., & de Lorgeril, M. (2014). Definitions and potential health benefits of the Mediterranean diet: views from experts around the world. BMC medicine, 12, 112. https://doi.org/10.1186/1741-7015-12-112

U.S. Department of Health and Human Services and U.S. Department of Agriculture. Dietary Guidelines for Americans 2015—2020, 8th Edition. December 2015. Accessed June 15, 2018. httrs://health.gov/dietarvzuide1ines/2015/guidelines/.

U.S. News & World Report. "Best Diets Overall." January 3, 2018. https://health.usnews.com/best-diet/best-diets-overall.

Made in United States
Troutdale, OR
11/17/2024